NORTH CASCADES

HIKING GUIDE 2025

A Detailed Manual Including Historic Sites,

Trails, Adventure Tips and more

ADELINE M. CREEL

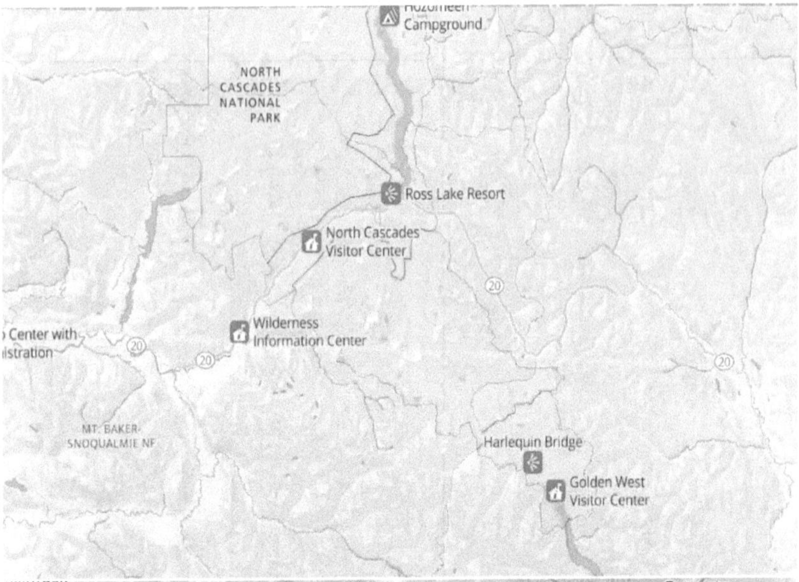
Campground
NORTH CASCADES NATIONAL PARK
Ross Lake Resort
North Cascades Visitor Center
20
Wilderness Information Center
MT. BAKER-SNOQUALMIE NF
Harlequin Bridge
Golden West Visitor Center

EC Manning Provincial Park
Eastgate
Glacier
Mt Shuksan
North Cascades National Park
Barron
Diablo
20
Newhalem
Concrete
Marblemount
Rockport
Gilbert

All Rights Reserved!

No part of this book may be reproduced, stored in a retrieval system, or transmitted in any form or by any means, electronic, mechanical, photocopying, recording, or otherwise, without the prior written permission of the copyright owner. Copyright 2025, Adeline M. Creel

DISCLAIMER

The content of this book is provided for informational purposes only. While the author has made every effort to ensure the accuracy and completeness of the information contained herein, the author assumes no responsibility for errors, omissions, or contradictions.

Any action you take upon the information in this book is strictly at your own risk. The author and publisher will not be held liable for any losses, damages, or injuries resulting from the use of this book or any reliance on the information provided. The opinions expressed in this book are those of the author and do not necessarily reflect the views of any organizations, institutions, or entities mentioned or affiliated with the content. Readers are encouraged to seek professional advice or conduct their own research where necessary.

Any references to people, locations, events, or organizations are for illustrative purposes only. Where real entities are referenced, they are used fictitiously unless explicitly stated. By reading this book, you agree to hold the author and publisher harmless from any claims, losses, or disputes that may arise in connection with your use of the information herein.

TABLE OF CONTENT

Introduction: A Wilderness Journey 9

Understanding: A Comprehensive Overview of The North Cascades Area 18

    Geography and Landscape 18

    The Special Environment: Plants and Animals 22

    The North Cascades' History and Culture 25

Planning Your Hike in The North Cascades 27

    The Best Time to Hike 27

    Budgeting for Your Hike 30

    Packing Essentials for Hiking in the North Cascades 33

    Travel documents 35

Essential Gear and Packing List for Hiking In The Northern Cascades 38

    Clothing and Footwear for North Cascades Hiking 39

    Navigation Tools: Maps, GPS, and Trail markers 41

    Food, Water, and Cooking Supplies 43

    Safety and Emergency Equipment 45

Easy Hikes in The North Cascades: Beginner-Friendly Trails With Beautiful Views 49

Moderate Trails for A Day Hike in The Northern Cascades 57

Challenging And Strenuous Hikes in The North Cascades: For the Bold and The Brave 64

Iconic Long-Distance and Multi-Day Hikes in The Northern Cascades 71

Camping And Overnight Stays in The North Cascades: A Guide to Sleeping In Nature 80

    Backcountry Camping Rules and Permits 81

    Top Campgrounds in the North Cascades 83

    Mountain Huts and Cabins for Overnight Stay 85

    Wild Camping Rules and Tips 87

A Hiker's Essential Guide to Safety and Navigation in The North Cascades 90

    Understanding Trail Markers and Signage 91

    Managing Unpredictable Weather Conditions 93

    Wildlife Safety for Bears, Cougars, and Other Animals 95

    Emergency Procedures and Rescue Service 97

Responsible And Sustainable Hiking in The Northern Cascades 99

    Leave No Trace Principles 100

    Respect for Local Communities and Indigenous Lands 103

    Environmentally Friendly Hiking Practices 104

    Conservation Efforts in the North Cascades 106

Seasonal Hiking in The North Cascades: A Guide to The Best Trails All Year Long 109

Summer Hiking (June to September): Peak Season for Adventure*110

Fall Foliage and Autumn Hiking (September to November): A Season of Color 112

Winter Hiking and Snowshoeing (December to March): A Frozen Wonderland 114

Spring Hiking and Wildflower Trails (March-May): The Rebirth of the Wilderness 116

Family And Group Hiking in The North Cascades: A Guide to Safe and Memorable Experiences 119

Top Family-Friendly Trails: Easy and Engaging Hikes for All Ages.120

Hiking with Pets: Rules and Tips for Exploring with Your Dog 123

Group Hiking Etiquette and Safety: Making the Experience Fun and Organized 125

Multi-Day and Advanced Hiking Adventures in The North Cascades 128

Hut-to-Hut Trekking in the North Cascades 129

Trail Running and Fastpacking: Covering Large Distances in the Backcountry 131

Alpine Hiking and Climbing Routes: Conquering Peaks 133

Crossing into Canada: International Hiking Trails 135

Practical Travel Tips for Exploring the North Cascades 138

Transportation to the North Cascades: Airports and Transit 139

Where to Stay: Hotels, Lodges, and Cabins 141

Where to Eat and Resupply While Hiking..143

Hidden Gems and Off-Beaten-Path Adventures 144

Conclusion: The End of The Trail, But Not the Adventure 147

Final thoughts and recommendations 148

APPENDIX 156

Useful Apps..156

Essential Travel Checklist for the North Cascades..........................159

Emergency Contacts for the North Cascades 161

Frequently Asked Questions 162

Travel Itineraries 164

Introduction: A Wilderness Journey

The North Cascades span Washington State's rough geography, providing a spectacular experience with craggy peaks, glacier-fed lakes, and deep valleys. Unlike many other hiking locations, this area is relatively unspoiled, allowing tourists to experience actual wilderness. With over two million acres of protected terrain, it is one of America's most remote and spectacular national parks. Hiking in the North Cascades is more than just following a trail; it's about immersing oneself in a location where nature sets the pace of life.

The aroma of pine wafts through the air, snow-capped peaks rise sharply against the sky, and crystal-clear streams wind through valleys brimming with wildflowers in the summer and golden leaves in the autumn.

Whether you're a casual day hiker or an experienced backpacker, the North Cascades offer a variety of trails, from short hikes to high-altitude climbs that will test even the most seasoned adventurer. Unlike the well-traveled routes of other recognized parks, the North Cascades are a hidden gem. Here, seclusion is not a luxury, but rather an expectation. The trails lead to alpine lakes that reflect the sky, waterfalls that roar down moss-covered cliffs, and ridgelines that appear to touch the clouds. The isolation of the terrain necessitates careful planning, but the result is a trekking experience that feels like going back in time—when nature was huge, wild, and uncontrolled.

Hiking in this region is both enjoyable and challenging. Trails frequently rise thousands of feet, providing views of steep mountains and ancient glaciers. The terrain is tough, with small trails, river crossings, and unpredictable weather.

Summer brings long days and vivid meadows, but the heat can be brutal at higher elevations. Autumn changes the slopes into flaming tones of red and gold, while winter hides the area in dense snow, rendering many pathways inaccessible.

Wildlife abounds, and interactions are part of the adventure. Marmots, mountain goats, and black bears live in these highlands. Hikers who appreciate nature can observe these species in their natural habitat. Streams and lakes supply clean water, but filtration is required to assure safety. Trail conditions change regularly, so hikers must be adaptable. The North Cascades require care, patience, and planning, yet the hiking experience here is unlike any other.

With hundreds of miles of trails, deciding where to begin can be difficult. Each path has its charm, whether it's a quick trip to a viewpoint or a multi-day trek through high alpine territory. The following are some of the most memorable walks in the North Cascades.

For those looking for a soft introduction to the area, these paths offer breathtaking scenery without demanding much effort.

Rainy Lake Trail This short but well-kept trail leads to a tranquil alpine lake surrounded by high cliffs. Golden larches contrast well with the blue lake in the autumn.

Washington Pass Overlook: A short trek rewards visitors with magnificent views of Liberty Bell Mountain and the neighboring summits.

Blue Lake Trail A moderate rise leads hikers to a stunning turquoise lake tucked between towering peaks. In the summer, the trail is lined with wildflowers, and in the fall, hikers may see the larch trees turn golden.

Maple Pass Loop This trail leads to a ridge with panoramic views of glacial valleys and craggy peaks, making it one of the most spectacular circuits in the area. In the autumn, the golden hues of larches form a breathtaking landscape.

Cascade Pass Trail This historic route, utilized by Indigenous groups and early explorers, ascends through lush meadows and switchbacks before opening out to a breathtaking view of jagged peaks.

Thunder Knob Trail This trek, which overlooks Diablo Lake, provides an outstanding combination of difficulty and reward while giving spectacular views of the emerald waters below.

These hikes provide an unforgettable backcountry experience for anyone willing to put their stamina to the test.

Sahale Arm Trail This strenuous climb takes hikers high above Cascade Pass, to a ridge with panoramic vistas and probable wildlife encounters, including mountain goats.

Hidden Lake Lookout After a strenuous trek through steep terrain, those who reach the summit are rewarded with a breathtaking view of Hidden Lake and a historic fire lookout that offers overnight stays.

Copper Ridge Loop This multi-day walk takes you through woods, ridgelines, and secluded valleys, providing an immersive wilderness experience.

Hiking in the North Cascades necessitates considerable planning. Many places lack cell coverage, and weather patterns can alter quickly. Packing the appropriate gear promotes both safety and comfort.

Clothing: Layering is crucial. A moisture-wicking base layer, an insulating mid-layer, and a waterproof shell defend against the unpredictable mountain weather.

Footwear To navigate rocky terrain and steep inclines, you'll need sturdy hiking boots with strong traction.

Navigation A comprehensive map, compass, or GPS device is required. Trails can be inadequately defined in some sections, making getting lost a serious possibility.

Food and Water Long hikes require high-energy snacks, a lightweight cooking burner, and a water filtering device.

First Aid Kit Always keep basic medical supplies in your pack, such as bandages, pain relievers, and emergency tools like a whistle and space blanket.

Summer Warm temperatures and long days make this the greatest time to hike, although afternoon thunderstorms can form swiftly.

Autumn Cooler weather and fewer tourists make fall an excellent time to explore, however, snow may fall unexpectedly at higher elevations.

Winter Heavy snowfall makes most trails unusable, but lower-elevation routes and snowshoeing options remain.

Spring Melting snow causes overflowing rivers and muddy conditions, making certain treks difficult.

Respecting animals is a component of responsible hiking. The North Cascades are home to black bears, deer, and smaller animals such as pikas and marmots. Maintaining a safe distance and carefully storing food decreases the likelihood of encounters.

Bear Safety Carrying bear spray, making noise when trekking, and putting food in bear-proof containers might help avoid unwelcome encounters.

Mountain Goats These animals are curious and may approach hikers. Giving them room promotes the safety of both people and wildlife.

Insects: Mosquitoes and biting insects can be a problem in the summer. Bringing bug repellant and wearing lightweight, long-sleeved clothing can assist in alleviating discomfort.

Camping is a great way to extend your journey and explore the wilderness. The park provides approved campgrounds as well as wilderness camping for those seeking privacy.

Campgrounds Areas such as Newhalem Creek and Colonial Creek have built campsites with modest amenities.

Backcountry Camping A permit is necessary for overnight stays in the backcountry. Campsites are sometimes first-come, first-served, so preparing ahead is critical.

Bear-Proof Storage: Hanging food or utilizing bear canisters protects both hikers and wildlife.

Hiking in the North Cascades is more than just an outdoor sport; it allows you to reconnect with nature in its purest form. The hardships of rocky paths, unexpected weather, and physical endurance are rewarded with breathtaking views of towering peaks and exquisite lakes that make every step worthwhile.

For those willing to embrace the wild, the North Cascades provide an experience that will linger with you long after the trek is over. Whether it's the seclusion of an isolated alpine ridge, the sound of a thundering waterfall, or the sight of a mountain goat perched on a rocky ledge, this terrain has an indelible impact.

Understanding: A Comprehensive Overview of The North Cascades Area

Geography and Landscape

One of the wildest and most breathtaking vistas in North America is created by the North Cascades, which span the northernmost parts of Washington State. This mountain range provides an unmatched wilderness experience with its rugged peaks, deep valleys, and enormous glaciers. This area offers a genuine backcountry experience because it is still relatively unknown to mass tourists, in contrast to the more well-known parks that draw sizable groups.

The range itself, which stretches from British Columbia in Canada to the southern region of Washington, is a rocky extension of the Cascade Mountains. More than 300 glaciers sculpt the terrain inside its borders, forming breathtaking icefalls and supplying water to innumerable rivers and lakes. An impressive skyline is created by the ragged peaks that rise high from the valley floors over thousands of years due to the unrelenting push of glaciers. Among these peaks are the imposing giants Mount Shuksan, Eldorado Peak, and the tall Mount Baker, a stratovolcano that dominates the range's western region.

The North Cascades are renowned for their harsh terrain, in contrast to the undulating foothills of other mountainous areas. Hiking in some valleys can be steep and difficult since they descend thousands of feet from the nearby ridgelines. The many lakes in the area—Diablo, Ross, and Baker, to mention a few—reflect the constantly shifting sky and their distinctive turquoise color comes from glacier runoff.

The North Cascades Highway (State Route 20), which passes through the mountains and serves as the only significant road access to the park's interior, splits this isolated wilderness in half. Once inside, however, pathways meander through alpine meadows, exposed peaks, and old forests, making it impossible to fully appreciate the landscape without walking.

Climate and Ideal Hiking Seasons

Because of the untamed alpine landscape and its closeness to the Pacific Ocean, the North Cascades see a wide variety of weather patterns. This area is characterized by quickly changing weather patterns that can transform a clear day into a stormy one in a matter of hours, in contrast to the drier, more consistent climates found in other hiking areas.

Seasons and Expectations

The spring season (March to May): The lower altitudes start to thaw as winter loosens its hold on the mountains, revealing roaring waterfalls and verdant surroundings. At higher elevations, however, snow persists far into May, rendering many trails impassable.

Access roads to isolated trailheads are frequently closed, and river crossings can be dangerous because of the melting snowpack.

June to September is summer. Due to the long daylight hours and generally stable weather, this is the most popular time of year for trekking. While the higher elevations stay cold even in the height of summer, alpine meadows are ablaze with wildflowers in July and August. But unexpected heat waves and thunderstorms can happen, especially in exposed places. Early in the season, snow can still be seen on some of the higher trails.

The fall season (September to November): The forests turn into a stunning display of reds, oranges, and yellows as the temperatures drop. Higher heights are home to larch trees, which turn a stunning gold before dropping their needles. With fewer people and clear, crisp days, this time of year provides some of the best hiking conditions. Snowfall, however, can start as early as October and swiftly cut off access at higher elevations.

Winter, which lasts from December to March: The North Cascades become a haven for seasoned winter hikers, snowshoers, and mountaineers while the landscape is covered in snow. Only those with the right gear and training should go into the backcountry, though, as avalanche danger is a continual worry. Until the next spring, many roads and trails are still closed. Because the climate in the area is unpredictable, preparedness is crucial. Hikers should always have emergency supplies, rain gear, and layers on hand in case of unexpected rains, even during the summer.

The Special Environment: Plants and Animals

One of the most varied ecosystems in the Pacific Northwest is found in the North Cascades, which are home to a variety of species, fragile alpine meadows, and tall old-growth forests. Different ecological zones are created by the region's sharp elevation variations, and each is teeming with a variety of rare plant and animal species.

Flora: The Vigorous and the Hardy

Forests in Lowlands: Dense forests of Douglas fir, western red cedar, and western hemlock predominate at lower elevations. An understory of ferns, mosses, and wild mushrooms is protected by the dense canopy of these centuries-old, towering trees. Delicate trilliums and colorful rhododendrons are among the amazing variety of plant life made possible by the damp environment.

Meadows in the subalpine region: The scenery changes to broad meadows that are a riot of color in the summertime above the tree line. The hillsides are covered in avalanche lilies, Indian paintbrush, and lupine, which draw both photographers and pollinators. When the wildflowers are at their height in mid-July, these places are especially beautiful.

Alpine Zone: Only hardy plants like heather, sedges, and lichens survive in the rocky terrain at the highest elevations, where vegetation becomes sparse. This area is dominated by glaciers and permanent snowfields, which contribute to its untamed beauty.

Fauna: Wild Life Experiences

A remarkable variety of creatures, some of which are uncommon elsewhere, can be found in the North Cascades.

Black Bears: These versatile animals forage for berries and insects as they wander through meadows and forests. Despite their general shyness, they should always be handled carefully.

It's crucial to store food properly and hike with bear awareness.

Goats in the Mountains: Hiker's love to see these nimble climbers, who are frequently seen along rocky ridgelines. Despite their seeming friendliness, they should not be approached because they can be erratic.

Pikas and Marmots: These little mammals live in the alpine zone, where they can be observed scuttling amid the stones or tanning on rocks. Their unique cries reverberate throughout the lowlands.

Cougars and Wolves: Both species are present in the area and are essential to preserving ecological equilibrium, although being hardly seen.

Predatory Birds: Peregrine falcons, great horned owls, and golden eagles patrol the skies, looking for movement below.

Because of the wide range of species present, every hike offers a chance to learn something new. The North Cascades provide a unique opportunity to experience nature in its most pristine state, whether you're seeing a black bear in the distance or hearing the bald eagle's cry overhead.

The North Cascades' History and Culture

Indigenous tribes flourished in the North Cascades long before European settlers arrived, and they had a strong connection to the land. For thousands of years, the Skagit, Nooksack, and Upper Similkameen peoples inhabited, hunted, and traversed these mountains, leaving behind traditions, tales, and pathways that are being followed today.

The North Cascades served as a spiritual and cultural fulcrum for these Indigenous people, in addition to being a physical location. They collected medicinal plants from the valley floors and fished for salmon in the Skagit and Stehekin Rivers, depending on the forests and rivers for their food. Seasonal migrations ensured sustainability and harmony with the natural world by following the land's rhythms.

Wide-ranging changes were brought about by the 19th-century entrance of European explorers. As homesteaders, fur traders, and gold prospectors traveled into the highlands, they uprooted Indigenous populations and changed the landscape. Roads and railroads were carved into formerly undeveloped land by the late 1800s, when logging and mining enterprises had started.

Early in the 20th century, when explorers and conservationists realized the area's unmatched beauty, the drive for protection got underway. The core of this wilderness was preserved while allowing for responsible exploration with the official creation of North Cascades National Park in 1968.

Both Indigenous and early colonial cultures' legacies are still interwoven with the area today. Names like Sahale Arm and Hozomeen Peak serve as reminders of the rich history ingrained in these mountains, and many trails trace historic pathways that were originally followed by early prospectors and Indigenous visitors.

More than just an outdoor sport, hiking in the North Cascades is a voyage through a landscape influenced by history and nature, where each step is a continuation of the trails taken by previous hikers.

Planning Your Hike in The North Cascades

The Best Time to Hike

The North Cascades change considerably with each season, providing unique hiking experiences depending on the time of year. Understanding seasonal changes is critical for both safety and enjoyment, as trails transition from lush, flower-filled meadows in summer to icy, unpredictable pathways in the colder months.

Spring (March-May): The Season of Transition

Spring is a season of awakening in the North Cascades, but it also brings obstacles. Snowmelt feeds tremendous waterfalls, and the lower valleys display early indications of vegetation. However, the higher altitudes stay buried in thick snow far into May, rendering many trails inaccessible. Melting ice causes creeks to rise, making crossing difficult, and certain paths may be impossible due to ice patches that remain. Lower-elevation trails, such as Thunder Knob or areas of the Skagit Valley, provide the finest conditions for hikers looking to start their hiking season early.

Summer (June-September): The Peak Hiking Season

Summer is the most reliable season for most hikers. By late June, the snowline has receded, revealing alpine meadows blooming with brilliant wildflowers. The days are long, the skies are frequently clear, and the landscape is at its most inviting. July and August are especially popular because of the pleasant weather and easy access to the trails.

However, people rise on well-known routes, and trailhead parking fills up rapidly. It is also the driest season; thus, certain water supplies may be lower than projected.

Autumn (September to November): A Hiker's Paradise

September brings a change to the North Cascades, when cooler air settles in and the landscape bursts with autumn colors. Larch trees turn a golden yellow, which contrasts well with the rocky mountain backdrop. With fewer hikers on the trails, now is one of the finest periods for seclusion. However, the weather can change quickly, and early snowfall at higher elevations may shut down key routes. Before starting out, it's a good idea to check the weather and trail conditions.

Winter (December-March): A Harsh Beauty

Winter turns the North Cascades into a wonderland of heavy snow and frozen lakes. While it is ideal for experienced outdoor hikers, trekking chances are limited. Traditional pathways have been replaced by snowshoeing and ski touring, and the possibility of an avalanche remains a concern.

Only individuals with the necessary equipment, avalanche expertise, and winter survival abilities should venture into the backcountry during this period.

Choosing the Best Time to Achieve Your Goals

For wildflowers and high-elevation hikes: July and August.

For less crowds and spectacular fall colors: Late September to early October.

For winter exploration and snowshoeing: December-March.

For lower-elevation hikes and waterfalls, April and May

Budgeting for Your Hike

Exploring the North Cascades can range from a low-cost trip to a more expensive excursion, depending on considerations such as lodging, transportation, and equipment. Careful planning ensures a flawless experience while keeping spending under control.

Permits and Parking Fees

One of the most significant benefits of hiking in the North Cascades is that most of the terrain is still open to explore.

There are no entrance fees for North Cascades National Park, however some areas in the adjacent recreation zones may require a permit.

Backcountry Camping Permits are required for overnight stays in selected wilderness zones. These are available in advance or at ranger stations, depending on the region.

Northwest Forest Pass Required for parking at several trailheads in the national forests that surround the park. A day pass is available; however, the yearly pass is more affordable for frequent visitors.

America the Beautiful Pass If you plan to visit many national parks and federal lands in a year, this pass grants admission to a variety of public sites across the United States.

Costs for Accommodation

Camping: The majority of campgrounds in the region charge $15 to $30 per night for a typical tent site. Backcountry camping permits are either free or for a modest price.

Lodges and Hotels: Prices range significantly, from low-cost motels in adjacent towns to pricier resorts near the park. Expect to pay anywhere between $80 and $300 per night.

Cabins and Vacation Rentals: A good alternative for people seeking greater comfort, with rates ranging from $100 to $400 per night, depending on the season.

Food and Supply

Grocery Costs: If you plan to prepare meals, set aside $10-$15 per person per day for basic trekking food.

Restaurant Meals: Dining in adjacent towns like Winthrop or Marblemount can cost anything from $12 for a casual dinner to $30+ at sit-down restaurants.

Trail Snacks: Lightweight, high-energy items such as almonds, granola bars, and freeze-dried dinners cost between $3 and $10 per item.

Transportation

Driving: Gas costs vary, but anticipate to spend between $50 and $100 on fuel, depending on your starting place and trip distance.

Public Transportation: There are limited bus services available, but having your own vehicle is the easiest way to get to trailheads.

Car Rentals: Rates vary, but typically begin at $40 per day, with additional surcharges for high-clearance or off-road capable vehicles.

Packing Essentials for Hiking in the North Cascades

Proper packing ensures that your trip to the North Cascades is safe and comfortable. The variable conditions necessitate careful planning, regardless of the season.

Clothes

Base Layers: Moisture-wicking fabrics keep sweat away from your skin.

Insulating Layers: For warmth, choose a fleece or lightweight down jacket.

Outer Shell: A waterproof, wind-resistant jacket is required.

Hiking Pants: Sturdy and breathable choices with waterproof shells for wet weather.

Gloves and Hat: Even in the summer, temperatures might fall abruptly.

Footwear

Hiking footwear: Durable, ankle-supporting footwear for rough terrain.

Camp Shoes: Lightweight footwear for relaxing in camp after a long trip.

Wool Socks: Helps avoid blisters and keeps feet toasty in any weather.

Gear

Backpack: A 20-30L pack for day hikes, and 50L or more for overnight trips.

Navigation: A physical map, compass, or GPS unit.

Trekking Poles: Provides stability on steep or uneven paths.

Headlamp: Required for early-morning starts or emergencies.

Emergency and Safety Items

First Aid Kit: Include bandages, pain relievers, antiseptic wipes, and any essential personal drugs.

Bear Spray: Bear spray is an absolute must-have for any bear encounter.

Emergency Shelter: A lightweight bivy bag or space blanket.

Multi-Tool: Ideal for short repairs and unexpected scenarios.

Travel documents

Most tourists' entry formalities are uncomplicated, but those traveling from abroad should plan accordingly.

Identification: US citizens should have a valid driver's license or passport.

Visitors from Canada: Crossing the border requires a passport or an improved driver's license.

Permits: If you camp overnight in the backcountry, you must have a wilderness permit.

Health and Safety Tip

Preventing Injury and Illness

Hydration: Drink plenty of water to stay hydrated, especially at higher elevations.

Altitude Awareness: Although the North Cascades do not reach severe heights, hikers may experience elevation increase. Acclimate gradually if necessary.

Prevent blisters by wearing moisture-wicking socks and footwear that have been properly broken in.

Wildlife Awareness

Bear Safety: Keep food in bear-proof containers, never approach bears, and carry bear spray.

Mountain Goat Behavior: These animals may approach hikers; keep a safe distance.

Ticks and Mosquitoes: Wear long sleeves and bug repellent during the peak summer months.

Emergency Preparation

Know Your Route: Before embarking on your journey, review trail maps.

Check Weather Forecasts: Be aware of potential storms, particularly in the afternoons.

Tell Someone Your Plans: Always inform a friend or family member of your schedule.

Hikers can plan ahead of time to ensure a memorable, safe, and pleasurable journey in the North Cascades. Whether taking on a calm lakeside walk or a difficult alpine trek, preparedness is essential for getting the most of this incredible landscape.

Essential Gear and Packing List for Hiking In The Northern Cascades

Exploring the North Cascades is an unforgettable adventure, but the difficult terrain necessitates careful preparation. The region's unpredictable weather, steep routes, and secluded nature necessitate those hikers prepare carefully to protect their safety and comfort. A well-planned kit list can make the difference between a good vacation and an unanticipated emergency.

Clothing and Footwear for North Cascades Hiking

Layering is required when hiking in the North Cascades since temperatures vary greatly between valleys and exposed ridgelines. Conditions can shift suddenly, with beautiful sky giving way to sudden downpour or frigid winds blowing across mountain passes.

Layering for comfort and protection

Base Layer: The initial layer should drain moisture away from your skin, allowing you to stay dry even when sweating. It is better to use lightweight merino wool or synthetic materials. Avoid cotton, which absorbs moisture and can cause chills.

Middle Layer: Insulates and maintains body heat. A fleece or down jacket is ideal for cooler weather since it provides warmth without adding unnecessary weight.

Outer Shell: A waterproof, windproof jacket is required. Rain is common in the North Cascades, and even a little drizzle might cause discomfort if you're not prepared.

Choose a breathable shell with pit zips to assist regulate body temperature.

Pant and Legwear

Hiking Pants: These pants are lightweight and easy to dry, making them suitable for most circumstances. Consider zip-off convertible pants for further flexibility.

Rain Pants: Waterproof pants are ideal for longer walks or high-altitude routes because they provide an extra layer of protection in the rain.

Thermal Base Layer: If hiking in colder weather or at higher elevations, insulated leggings or wool tights will assist keep you warm.

Footwear for Stability and Comfort in Rough Terrain

Hiking Boots: Strong boots with ankle support are required for navigating rocky routes and steep inclines. Look for waterproof models with a firm grip for navigating wet or lose ground.

Trail Runners: Ideal for well-kept trails or shorter excursions, these offer comfort and flexibility while remaining lightweight.

Gaiters: Gaiters are useful in muddy or snowy circumstances as they keep dirt, water, and debris out of your boots.

Socks: Merino wool socks help regulate temperature and avoid blisters. Packing an additional pair keeps your feet dry during the hike.

Navigation Tools: Maps, GPS, and Trail markers

The North Cascades are large, with numerous trails across the terrain. Cell service is unreliable; thus, it is critical to bring suitable navigation gear to avoid getting lost.

Physical Map and Compass

Topographic Maps: A printed map from a reputable source, such as the National Park Service or the USGS, has precise information about elevation, trails, and landmarks.

Compass: Even if you're using a GPS gadget, a compass is a must-have backup in case the battery fails. Knowing how to read a map and orient yourself with a compass is essential for backcountry exploration.

GPS and Digital Tools

Handheld GPS gadget: A GPS gadget is dependable and suited for harsh situations; it can trace your trip and assist you find your way back if necessary.

Smartphone Apps: Apps like Gaia GPS, AllTrails, and Topo Maps+ provide offline maps, but battery life must be carefully controlled. If you rely on digital navigation, always keep a backup charging solution handy.

Trailmarkers and Signs

While some well-traveled paths are clearly marked, many routes in the North Cascades are remote and lightly maintained. Pay special attention to cairns, trailblazers, and signposts where they are available. In locations with few markings, maintaining a sharp awareness of your surroundings is important to staying on track.

Food, Water, and Cooking Supplies

A well-fueled body is vital for handling steep hills and long hikes. The correct meal and hydration approach can significantly improve energy levels and endurance.

Food for the trail

High-Energy Snacks: Nuts, dried fruit, energy bars, and jerky provide rapid energy without adding unnecessary weight to your pack.

Freeze-Dried Meals: These meals are lightweight and quick to make, requiring only boiling water and containing a balanced mix of carbohydrates, proteins, and fats.

Nut Butters and Tortillas: Combining peanut butter or almond butter with tortillas or crackers creates a simple, high-calorie lunch.

Instant Oatmeal: An excellent breakfast alternative that takes little cooking and gives long-lasting energy.

Water: How to Stay Hydrated in the Wilderness

Reliable water sources are available throughout the North Cascades, however drinking directly from streams or lakes is not recommended due to the risk of waterborne diseases.

Water Filtration System: A portable water filter or purification tablets provide clean drinking water.

Hydration Reservoir or Bottles: A hydration bladder (like a CamelBak) provides convenient access to water while trekking, whilst foldable water bottles save space.

Cooking and Food Preparation

Lightweight Stove: A tiny camping stove, such as the Jetboil or MSR PocketRocket, allows you to boil water quickly and efficiently.

Fuel Canisters: Make sure you have adequate fuel for the duration of your journey, as refill sites are limited.

Cookware: A lightweight pot, spork, and collapsible bowl make meal preparation easier.

Fire Safety: Open fires are frequently restricted in remote locations, so always check the rules before cooking over an open flame.

Safety and Emergency Equipment

Due to the isolation of the North Cascades, hikers must carry critical safety equipment to deal with unexpected emergencies.

First Aid Kit: Prepare for Minor Injuries

- A compact, well-stocked first aid pack should contain:
- bandages and blister pads.
- Antiseptic wipes, antibiotic ointment
- Pain relief and antihistamines
- Tweezers for removing splinters and ticks.
- Emergency blanket for sudden chilly weather
- Personal meds (as needed).

Emergency Signalling Devices

Whistle: A simple but efficient strategy to indicate distress if lost or injured.

Mirror or Reflective Device: Can be used to alert rescuers in daylight.

Personal Locator Beacon (PLB): In severe instances, a PLB or satellite messenger (such as a Garmin inReach) allows you to call for assistance in locations without cell coverage.

Shelter and Protection from The Elements

Carrying an emergency shelter is a good idea even if you don't plan on staying overnight.

Lightweight Tent or Bivy Sack: Offers protection in the event of an unforeseen delay or injury.

Space Blanket: reflects body heat and can be used as a temporary survival gear.

Bear and Wildlife Safety

The North Cascades are home to black bears, so take steps to prevent interactions.

Bear Canister or Ursack: Required in some places, these protect food from bears and rats.

Bear Spray: A last resort deterrent in the event of an aggressive encounter. Always understand how to use it appropriately.

Multi-tool and repair kit

A tiny multi-tool including a knife, pliers, and screwdrivers can be extremely useful for repairing broken gear, cutting rope, and dealing unforeseen repairs.

Headlamp with Extra Batteries

Even if you're planning a day trek, packing a headlamp ensures vision in case of delays. A lightweight LED variant with extra batteries is recommended.

Weather Protection

Sunscreen and Sunglasses: High-altitude exposure raises UV danger, especially on cloudy days.

Bug Repellent: Mosquitoes may be merciless in the summer. DEET-containing sprays or natural alternatives can help prevent bites.

Hiking in the North Cascades is an unforgettable experience, but preparation is essential for staying safe and enjoying the expedition. Hikers may confidently explore remote trails if they bring the proper clothing, food, and emergency supplies. The wildness in this region is spectacular, but it requires respect and cautious planning. With the proper equipment, you can fully appreciate the beauty and hardships of these mountains, resulting in a memorable and gratifying adventure.

Easy Hikes in The North Cascades: Beginner-Friendly Trails with Beautiful Views

For those wishing to visit the North Cascades without committing to a rigorous climb, the region has a number of trails that provide stunning scenery without requiring significant elevation gain or technical experience. Whether you're looking for a calm woodland walk, a short climb to a stunning overlook, or a leisurely stroll along a glacial lake, these beginner-friendly routes provide a wonderful introduction to one of the most remote mountain ranges in the United States.

Each of these walks provides an up-close look at the beauty of the North Cascades while remaining accessible to hikers of all skill levels.

Rainy Lake Trail: Short Walk to Tranquility

Distance: 2 kilometers round way.

Elevation Gain: Minimal.

Trailhead: Rainy Pass (Highway 20)

For those looking for a relaxing walk with an outstanding view at the end, the Rainy Lake Trail is an excellent choice. This well-kept paved route leads to a breathtaking alpine lake surrounded by towering cliffs and flowing waterfalls.

The hike starts at Rainy Pass, where a pleasant track leads through a lovely woodland with towering firs and moss-covered boulders. As you travel, the sound of running water accompanies you, hinting of the lake ahead. Within a mile, the forests give way to expose the glittering waters of Rainy Lake, flanked by craggy peaks coated with snow, even in the warmer months.

The tranquil environment invites trekkers to take in the landscape. Bring a picnic or just relax by the shore and listen to the odd splash of a fish breaking the surface. In the autumn, golden larches add a magnificent burst of color, making this one of the North Cascades' most photogenic places.

Rainy Lake is great for families, first-time hikers, and those searching for a brief but stunning getaway into nature.

Blue Lake Trail: A Short Climb to a Stunning Alpine Lake

Distance: 4.4-mile round trip.

Elevation Gain: 1,050 ft.

Trailhead: Near Washington Pass.

Blue Lake is one of the most accessible alpine lakes in the North Cascades, so it's a must-do for people looking for a slightly longer trip without too much difficulty. Though this trail has significant elevation gain, the easy switchbacks and moderate gradient make it ideal for beginners looking for a little challenge.

The hike starts in a deep subalpine forest, with the path meandering by little streams and wildflower meadows. As the trail climbs, glimpses of rugged peaks appear through the woods, providing a sample of the scenery ahead. After around two miles, the trail levels off and the shimmering Blue Lake appears, its blue waters mirroring the surrounding rocks.

This pristine alpine setting is ideal for a lunch break, photography, or simply admiring the tranquil splendor of the high country. In late summer, wildflowers blossom along the coastline, and in autumn, golden larch trees create a fiery contrast to the deep blue of the lake.

This hike is relatively short and well-marked, making it an excellent introduction to the North Cascades' alpine scenery for those without expert hiking skills.

Thunder Knob Trail: A Stunning View Above Diablo Lake

Distance: 3.6-mile round trip.

Elevation Gain: 635 ft.

Trailhead: Colonial Creek Campground.

The Thunder Knob Trail provides one of the nicest views in the North Cascades with minimal effort. This moderate, beginner-friendly journey takes you through old-growth forests and over a gradual hill, culminating in a beautiful view of Diablo Lake, famed for its spectacular emerald-green waters.

Starting at Colonial Creek Campground, the trail starts flat before gradually ascending through a shady woodland of firs and cedars. Before ascending to the overlook, you'll cross a few tiny rivers and pass over mossy boulders.

At the summit, a panoramic view of Diablo Lake and the surrounding mountains opens before you. The vivid waterways, tinted by glacial sediment, seem stunning against the dark green trees and rocky peaks. This is a great site to snap photos or just relax and enjoy the view.

Because of the moderate elevation rise, this is an excellent trip for novices who want to experience some climbing without being overwhelmed. It's also one of the best short hikes for seeing the sunset since the golden light over the lake produces a stunning panorama.

Washington Pass Overlook: A Short Walk with Big Rewards

Distance: 0.3 mile round trip.

Elevation Gain: Negative.

Trailhead: Washington Pass.

For those who want to see the magnificence of the North Cascades without a long hike, the Washington Pass Overlook is an excellent choice. This paved path leads to an outstanding viewpoint that overlooks the spectacular peaks of Washington Pass, including the iconic Liberty Bell Mountain.

A short walk from the parking lot leads to a wooden platform located on the edge of a sheer cliff, with breathtaking views of the valley below. Even though this is not a standard hike, the scenery is some of the most stunning in the area, making it a must-see for first-time tourists and those who aren't ready for a long trek.

This viewpoint is especially beautiful in the early morning or late afternoon when shifting light creates dramatic shadows across the craggy mountains. It's also a great site for wildlife watching, since mountain goats may be spotted mounting the neighboring cliffs.

Ladder Creek Falls Trail is a short hike through a hidden gorge.

Distance: 0.5-mile round trip.

Elevation Gain: Minimal.

Trailhead: Near the Gorge Powerhouse in Newhalem.

Ladder Creek Falls is a unique and lesser-known trek that takes you on a short but lovely excursion through a lush rainforest-like setting. This walk, located near the village of Newhalem, takes you into a narrow ravine where cascading waterfalls flow over moss-covered rocks.

The walk starts at Gorge Powerhouse and crosses a suspension bridge before winding through a grove of tall trees and bright ferns. At night, the falls are lit up with colorful lights, providing a wonderful ambiance.

While short, this trail offers an intimate glimpse into the beauty of the North Cascades' lower-elevation forests, making it an excellent stop for families or those looking for a brief and picturesque walk. The North Cascades are frequently associated with strenuous alpine hikes, but as these trails demonstrate, other beginner-friendly options deliver incredible beauty without undue effort. Whether you're looking over the surreal waters of Diablo Lake, meandering through flower-filled meadows, or exploring hidden waterfalls, these treks provide the ideal introduction to the magic of the North Cascades.

Each of these pathways demonstrates that you don't have to embark on a strenuous climb to appreciate the raw beauty of this mountainous nature. Hikers of all skill levels can discover a trail that fits their pace while still providing unforgettable views with a little planning and a sense of adventure.

Moderate Trails for A Day Hike in The Northern Cascades

The North Cascades are noted for their secluded wildness, jagged peaks, and spectacular scenery. While some trails need technical expertise and multi-day treks, numerous moderate day hikes strike the ideal combination of work and reward. These paths offer just enough challenge to keep things interesting, while also allowing hikers to take in vast mountain views, crystal-clear alpine lakes, and diverse terrain in a single day.

The following walks provide some of the nicest scenery in the North Cascades for those seeking an adventure that involves a little more climbing and a touch of seclusion without demanding expert-level stamina.

Maple Pass Loop: A Grand Circuit with Endless Views.

Distance: 7.2-mile loop

Elevation Gain: 2,200 ft.

Trailhead: Rainy Pass (Highway 20)

Maple Pass, regarded as one of the most stunning loops walks in the North Cascades, has everything a hiker might desire—wildflower meadows, towering ridgelines, glistening lakes, and vast views that span kilometers.

The trail begins at Rainy Pass, where hikers can choose to complete the loop clockwise or counterclockwise. Many people choose to go counterclockwise because it provides for a gentler rise and a magnificent, jaw-dropping view of the North Cascades' craggy peaks as you climb higher.

The first several miles pass through dense forests, with views of Rainy Lake below. As the track ascends, it opens into a broad alpine basin teeming with seasonal wildflowers in June and golden larches in autumn. The final push to the top leads hikers to a ridge with unbroken views of craggy mountains such as Black Peak and Corteo Peak. Despite the trail's steady rise, the well-maintained path and constant scenery changes make it one of the most enjoyable moderate treks in the area. The descent provides equally amazing views, making each step of this loop worthwhile.

Cascade Pass Trail: A Historical and Scenic Climb

Distance: 7.4 miles round trip.

Elevation Gain: 1,800 ft.

Trailhead: Cascade River Road

Few paths in the North Cascades provide as much scenic reward for moderate effort as Cascade Pass. This trail, once used by Indigenous travelers and early explorers, follows an old route that passes through lush meadows and glacier-carved valleys before arriving at one of the park's most famous vistas.

The trail starts with gentle switchbacks and gradually takes walkers into a forest filled with towering firs and hemlocks. As you ascend, the sound of falling streams becomes more audible, and the trees thin out, offering a stunning panorama of glacial valleys and soaring peaks.

At the pass, the panorama unfolds in all directions, revealing Johannesburg Mountain, the massive Eldorado Glacier, and the stunning cliffs of the Stehekin Valley. It is not uncommon to see marmots sunbathing on the rocks or hear the distant call of a ptarmigan in the alpine tundra.

For those seeking more challenge, the pass provides a portal to Sahale Arm, a more difficult extension with an even more beautiful landscape. However, for those who stick to the main trail, the climb is more than worthwhile, providing one of the best panoramic views in the North Cascades.

Hidden Lake Lookout Trail: A Staircase to the Sky

Distance: 8 kilometers round trip.

Elevation Gain: 3,300 ft.

Trailhead: Near Marblemount.

For those wishing to push the limits of a moderate hike, Hidden Lake Lookout provides a spectacular mix of woodland, alpine meadows, rocky ridgelines, and a historic fire lookout.

The trail begins pleasantly enough, passing past lush foliage and streams trickling down from snowfields above. The switchbacks quickly become steeper, leading hikers to an open meadow overflowing with wildflowers in the summer. The true difficulty comes as the trail climbs toward a rocky pass, with sweeping views of the surrounding peaks** opening up in every direction.

Hikers are rewarded at the top with a spectacular view of Hidden Lake, which has turquoise waters hidden within a deep glacial basin. On a clear day, you can see as far as Mount Baker and the distant summits of the Olympic Mountains.

A final scramble leads to the Hidden Lake Fire Lookout, a renovated ranger station with 360-degree views of the Cascade Range. While getting to the lookout takes some effort, the strange experience of being on the edge of the world makes it one of the most memorable climbs in the park.

Chain Lakes Loop: A Relaxing Journey Through High Alpine Terrain

Distance: 7-mile loop.

Elevation Gain: 1,800 ft.

Trailhead: Artist Point.

For those who desire a variety of sceneries without a hard climb, the Chain Lakes Loop is the ideal choice. This walks near Mount Baker winds past a series of stunning alpine lakes and provides frequent views of snow-capped summits and wildflower-strewn meadows. Starting at Artist Point, the walk descends to Bagley Lakes, two crystalline ponds that reflect the surrounding mountains. A moderate climb takes you to Herman Saddle, where the horizon unfolds in every direction, revealing views of Mount Shuksan, Table Mountain, and the distant peaks of British Columbia.

The trail then continues through the Chain Lakes, a series of glacial-fed ponds set against a rugged backdrop of cliffs and glaciers. Along the route, you may see mountain goats grazing on the ridgelines or golden marmots scurrying between the boulders.

This hike stands out for its diverse terrain—rocky ridges, wildflower meadows, alpine lakes, and towering peaks all packed into a single loop. Because of its moderate elevation gain and well-maintained paths, this hike is an excellent introduction to high-country trekking without overwhelming effort. For those wishing to experience the best of the North Cascades without attempting the region's most arduous hikes, these moderate routes provide the perfect middle ground. Each one provides a variety of mountain views, unique landscapes, and gratifying challenges in a single day.

Whether standing at the summit of Cascade Pass, staring over the mirror-like surface of Chain Lakes, or climbing to the sky at Hidden Lake Lookout, these paths remind hikers why the North Cascades remain one of North America's most untamed and breathtaking wilderness areas.

With a sense of adventure and a well-packed daypack, these picturesque paths allow hikers to experience the grandeur of the North Cascades—without having to spend many days in the backcountry.

Challenging And Strenuous Hikes in The North Cascades: For the Bold and The Brave

The North Cascades provide some of the most challenging and rewarding hikes in the Pacific Northwest. Unlike easy-going trails, which deliver picturesque benefits with no exertion, these strenuous routes require endurance, strength, and mental tenacity. The benefits, however, are beyond measure—towering peaks, limitless ridgelines, glacier-fed lakes, and a sense of satisfaction that only comes from conquering the most difficult terrain. For those seeking a challenge, these hikes test both physical stamina and mental tenacity.

These routes are suitable for experienced hikers wishing to take their North Cascades trip to the next level, with steep climbs, exposed ridgelines, and extended ascents.

Sahale Arm Trail: The High-Alpine Dream

Distance: 12 miles roundtrip.

elevation gain: 4,000 feet

Trailhead: Cascade Pass.

The Sahale Arm Trail is one of the most breathtaking and strenuous walks in the North Cascades, leading to a world of snow-capped peaks, sweeping meadows, and glacier-fed wonders. The journey begins at Cascade Pass and continues through a series of relentless switchbacks through deep forests until arriving in an open valley. The climb is abrupt and unyielding, yet with each step, the vista becomes more stunning. Once at Cascade Pass, the true test begins. The trail winds through a high-alpine wonderland, where marmots bask on rocky outcroppings and fields of wildflowers burst into color throughout the summer months. The final push to Sahale Glacier Camp is a hard, rocky slope that leads to one of the most stunning views in the entire North Cascades.

From this vantage position, the jagged summits of Forbidden Peak and Mount Buckner rise in every direction, while Sahale Glacier flows over the ridgeline. The vistas spread for miles, making the difficult climb well worth it.

This hike is not for the faint of heart because the ascent is relentless and exposed. However, for those who are willing to face the challenge, the benefits are nothing short of amazing.

Hidden Lake Lookout: A Staircase to the Sky

Distance: 8 kilometers round trip.

Elevation Gain: 3,300 ft.

Trailhead: Near Marblemount.

The Hidden Lake Lookout trail, located high above a pristine alpine lake, is both hard and lovely. This hike, known for steep climbs and exposed terrain, tests endurance and determination. The first segment winds through a deep forest, and the incline is instantly apparent. There is no gradual incline—this trail is difficult from the beginning.

As the woods thin out, hikers encounter an open meadow filled with wildflowers before taking on the final, grueling ascent across boulder fields and scree slopes.

At the summit, the Hidden Lake Fire Lookout sits on a rocky ridge, affording 360-degree views of the North Cascades. Below, Hidden Lake is surrounded by high peaks and sparkles of icy blue. On a clear day, Mount Baker, Eldorado Peak, and distant glaciers are visible on the horizon.

Though this hike requires a lot of energy, the views from the top make it all worthwhile. Those seeking an additional challenge can cautiously descend to the lake itself—a steep, off-trail scramble that needs steady footing and solid experience.

Desolation Peak: A Climb into Literary History

Distance: 9.4 miles round trip.

Elevation Gain: 4,400 ft.

Trailhead: Ross Lake.

Few treks in the North Cascades can match Desolation Peak for a sense of solitude.

With a constant incline and no easy sections, this trail is a battle against gravity from start to finish.

The top, which was made famous by writer Jack Kerouac, who spent a summer here as a fire lookout in the 1950s, offers incredible views of Ross Lake and the surrounding mountains. The trail starts along the shoreline and climbs aggressively through thick forests to reach the ridgeline. From here, hikers must push over exposed switchbacks, frequently fighting wind and unpredictable weather.

The summit lookout, which is still in use today, offers an iconic setting for reflection—a spot where mountain ridges dissolve into the horizon, and the seclusion of the wilderness becomes genuinely apparent. The descent is nearly as difficult as the climb, with continuous stress on the knees, thus trekking poles are highly suggested.

For those wishing to experience the North Cascades in its rawest form, Desolation Peak provides an unfiltered glimpse into the region's majesty and beauty.

Copper Ridge Loop is a multi-day challenge

Distance: 34 miles round trip.

Elevation Gain: 7,000 ft.

Trailhead: Hannegan Pass

For hikers looking to push beyond a single-day challenge, Copper Ridge Loop is one of the most spectacular and difficult multi-day hikes in the North Cascades. This backcountry odyssey takes you across inaccessible ridgelines, high-mountain passes, and deep glacier valleys.

The first leg steadily ascends toward Hannegan Pass, providing expansive views of Mount Shuksan. From there, the trail traverses Copper Ridge, where hikers may enjoy some of the park's finest uninterrupted mountain scenery. Glacier Peak, Mount Redoubt, and other ridgelines extend far into the distance.

The descent to the Chilliwack River Valley is lengthy and difficult, with several river crossings and steep descents. This rugged and remote stretch of the trip demonstrates why the

North Cascades are one of the least-traveled wilderness areas in the country.

This track requires extensive backcountry experience, but for those ready to take on the task, the rewards are nothing short of world-class.

The North Cascades aren't meant to be conquered easy. These difficult walks require resilience, endurance, and respect for the elements. Every summit, ridgeline, and glacial lake discovered is gained through effort, sweat, and determination.

For those wanting an extraordinary experience, these paths offer more than just stunning scenery—they give a sense of accomplishment, a deep connection to the wilderness, and a story to carry long after the adventure ends.

Iconic Long-Distance and Multi-Day Hikes in The Northern Cascades

The North Cascades are home to some of the most challenging and breathtaking terrain in the United States. Unlike shorter day walks, which provide a peek at the region's magnificence, long-distance and multi-day treks take hikers deep into the mountains. These paths run through remote valleys, high mountain passes, glacier-fed rivers, and unspoiled forests, rewarding those who are willing to face the task with some of North America's most stunning scenery.

For those wishing to experience the true backcountry and spend many days immersed in nature, these long-distance hikes are unrivaled in beauty and adventure.

The Ptarmigan Traverse: A High-Alpine Odyssey.

Distance: 35+ miles.

Elevation Gain: 12,000+ ft.

Trailhead: Cascade Pass.

The Ptarmigan Traverse is not simply a hike, but an expedition. This legendary high route traverses some of the most remote and glaciated terrain in the North Cascades, necessitating technical mountaineering skills, route-finding abilities, and full self-reliance.

Starting at Cascade Pass, the journey swiftly leaves the trail behind and enters a realm of everlasting snowfields, craggy peaks, and stunning ice formations. Each step leads hikers deeper into an alpine wilderness unspoiled by roads or contemporary conveniences.

The trek entails climbing over many glaciers, including Le Conte, South Cascade, and Dome Glacier, making it a serious undertaking only for experienced mountaineers.

The vistas along the road are unrivaled, with towering peaks such as Formidable, Sinister, and Dome Peak dominating the landscape. Camp sites are frequently located on high ridges or adjacent to glacial lakes, providing perfect isolation under the stars.

For those with the expertise, endurance, and fortitude to embark on this legendary traverse, the experience is nothing short of transformative.

Copper Ridge Loop: A Journey in the High Country

Distance: 34 miles.

Elevation Gain: 7,000+ ft.

Trailhead: Hannegan Pass

The Copper Ridge Loop is one of the North Cascades' most magnificent multi-day treks, featuring dramatic ridgeline trekking, river crossings, and breathtaking views of glaciated peaks.

The path begins at Hannegan Pass and climbs through lush wildflower-filled meadows in summer before reaching the high alpine peaks. As hikers rise, the vistas expand to a never-ending sea of mountain peaks, with Mount Shuksan and Mount Baker towering tall in the distance.

This trek's highlight is the Copper Ridge Lookout, one of the region's most remote and magnificent fire lookouts. From this vantage point, glaciers flow down mountainsides, and Canada's craggy peaks stretch far beyond the horizon.

Hikers descend into the Chilliwack River Valley, where they meet a radically different landscape—old-growth woods, roaring rivers, and wildlife-rich lowlands. Black bears are commonly observed here, and the sense of remoteness is palpable.

With its mix of high-alpine terrain and deep valley crossings, this loop offers one of the most diverse and rewarding backpacking experiences in the North Cascades.

Devil's Dome Loop is a high-elevation masterpiece.

Distance: 40 miles.

Elevation Gain: 8,000+ ft.

Trailhead: Ross Lake

The Devil's Dome Loop offers dramatic ridgelines, panoramic mountain views, and real backcountry solitude. This challenging path provides one of the best long-distance ridge walks in the entire North Cascades, with near-constant views of jagged peaks, glacial valleys, and the deep blue waters of Ross Lake.

The journey starts with a steady ascent through dense forest, which finally leads to open alpine meadows where marmots sunbathe on boulders and eagles soar overhead. As hikers travel higher, the ridgeline opens up, providing a spectacular 360-degree view of the surrounding environment.

One of the most memorable sections is the stretch across Devil's Dome when hikers walk along an exposed ridge with nothing but sky and mountains in all directions.

This is true alpine hiking, where the grandeur of the environment inspires feelings of insignificance and awe.

After several days in the highlands, the trail gradually descends to Ross Lake, where the peaceful waters contrast sharply with the rocky heights above. The loop takes strong endurance and backcountry abilities, but the benefits are immeasurable for those who embrace the challenge.

The Pasayten Wilderness Traverse is a remote backcountry gem.

Distance: 50 to 80 miles, depending on the route

Elevation Gain: varies.

Trailhead: Multiple entry places.

The Pasayten Wilderness is one of the least-traveled yet most spectacular sections of the North Cascades. This huge stretch of wilderness, covering more than half a million acres, is home to rolling ridgelines, wide meadows, and deep, forested valleys that feel completely undisturbed.

Unlike many other North Cascades treks, the Pasayten Wilderness Traverse offers a distinct type of beauty—instead of sharp, glaciated peaks, this route boasts wide-open ridges that stretch for miles, giving some of the most magnificent sunsets in the Pacific Northwest.

Hikers can create their custom route by connecting routes that pass-through highlights like:

Frosty Pass - A stunning mountain crossing with panoramic views.

Tungsten Mine - A remarkable abandoned mining site located deep in the countryside.

Larch Pass- Best visited in the autumn, when the golden larch trees illuminate the hillsides.

Because of its remoteness, the Pasayten Wilderness is ideal for people seeking solitude. With few hikers, huge open expanses, and plentiful wildlife, this route provides a true sensation of escape.

The Pacific Crest Trail via the North Cascades

Distance: More than 125 kilometers through the park

Elevation Gain: Constant elevation changes.

Trailhead: Multiple entry places.

For those seeking to explore one of the most famous long-distance trails in the world, the Pacific Crest Trail (PCT) segment through the North Cascades is a memorable adventure.

This section of the PCT passes through some of the most breathtaking scenery in the park, including remote valleys, alpine lakes, and sky-scraping peaks. Highlights include:

Glacier Peak Wilderness - A spectacular region with towering peaks and glacial rivers.

Cutthroat Pass - A breathtaking high-mountain trek that feels like it leads to another world. Rainy Pass to the Canadian Border - The final section of the PCT provides awe-inspiring ridge treks and deep solitude.

Hikers can opt to complete smaller sections of the trail** or the whole North Cascades segment, which provides a world-class long-distance trek through one of the most untamed landscapes in the United States.

For those who enjoy the raw force of the wilderness, the North Cascades provide some of the most challenging and rewarding long-distance walks in the country. These paths require labor, preparation, and perseverance—but the sense of success and stunning views make every arduous mile worthwhile.

Whether climbing over glaciers, trekking high-alpine ridgelines, or sleeping beneath the stars in perfect solitude**, these multi-day journeys deliver an experience that lasts long after the boots are removed and the packs are unpacked.

For those who dare to go, the North Cascades will leave an indelible stamp on the soul.

Camping And Overnight Stays in The North Cascades: A Guide to Sleeping In Nature

Spending the night in the North Cascades is a truly unique experience. As the sun sets below rocky peaks and the last golden light fades over glacier lakes, the environment changes into a world of complete quiet. Whether you're camping deep in the backcountry, resting in a quaint mountain hut, or pitching a tent along a beautiful lake, overnight stays in the North Cascades provide an unrivaled connection to nature.

However, with great beauty comes responsibility. The remoteness of this region necessitates proper planning, adherence to regulations, and knowledge of Leave No Trace principles. This handbook includes everything you need to know about camping in the North Cascades, including permits and regulations and the greatest campsites and hidden backcountry gems.

Backcountry Camping Rules and Permits

The North Cascades protect some of the most fragile wilderness in the Pacific Northwest, thus strong rules exist to preserve the scenery and assure visitor safety.

Wilderness Camping Permit

For individuals visiting backcountry areas, a wilderness camping permit is necessary for any overnight stay. These permits aim to limit human impact on the ecosystem by requiring hikers to camp in approved locations that safeguard wildlife and plants.

Where to Get a Permit?

Available on the National Park Service website or in person at the Wilderness Information Centers in Marblemount and Glacier.

Reservations for popular routes, such as Sahale Glacier Camp or Cascade Pass, should be booked in advance, particularly during the high summer months.

Permit Free Areas:

Some national forest lands next to the park do not require permits, but campers should always verify local rules before setting out.

Leave No Trace and Campfire Rules

The fragile alpine environment of the North Cascades cannot recover fast from human activity.

Campfires are prohibited at high elevations and in sensitive alpine areas to protect fragile ecosystems.

Rather than burning wood, campers should utilize lightweight stoves for cooking.

All waste, including food scraps and hygiene items, must be packed out.

By following these guidelines, visitors can help conserve the pristine wilderness for future generations while also assuring the safety of hikers and wildlife.

Top Campgrounds in the North Cascades

For those who prefer a basecamp experience with access to roads and basic facilities, the North Cascades' established campgrounds offer comfort without sacrificing the wilderness feel.

Colonial Creek Campground, Diablo Lake Area

Best For: Lakeside camping, kayaking, and convenient trail access.

Reservations: Yes, in high season.

Amenities: Restrooms, picnic tables, and boat launch.

Colonial Creek, located beside the shimmering turquoise waters of Diablo Lake, is one of the North Cascades' finest scenic front-country campgrounds. It has convenient access to Thunder Knob Trail and Ross Lake, making it a perfect location for campers looking to explore without going too far into the backcountry.

Newhalem Creek Campground

Perfect for: Families, RV camping, and proximity to visitor centers

Reservations are recommended during peak months.

Amenities: Restrooms, drinking water, and picnic tables

Located in Newhalem, this campground is ideal for people seeking a gentler introduction to the North Cascades. It allows access to short walks, gorgeous overlooks, and historic sites while yet providing the tranquil pleasure of sleeping beneath towering evergreens.

Hozomeen Campground (Ross Lake Area).

Best For: solitude, tough campsites, and access to Ross Lake.

No reservations; first-come, first-served.

Amenities: Pit toilets, rustic campsites (no water or connections).

For those willing to venture off the main path, Hozomeen provides true seclusion. This campground, which can only be reached by boat or a long drive through Canada, is far distant from civilization, making it ideal for wilderness lovers seeking an immersive experience.

Mountain Huts and Cabins for Overnight Stay

For those who prefer the mountain experience without a tent, several historic fire lookouts, huts, and cabins offer a primitive yet unforgettable overnight stay in the North Cascades.

Hidden Lake Lookout

Perfect for: High-altitude views and astronomy

Reservations: First come, first served.

Amenities: No facilities; carry everything you need.

Perched on a rocky peak overlooking Hidden Lake, this historic fire lookout gives some of the most breathtaking overnight views in the park. Hikers who reach the top can sleep inside the little wooden cabin, which is available to the public on a first-come, first-served basis.

Sahale Glacier Camp

Best For: Serious travelers and alpine enthusiasts.

Reservations are required.

Amenities: None—backcountry camping only

This high-elevation campsite lies on the edge of Sahale Glacier and provides one of the most surreal dawn and sunset experiences in the North Cascades. Accessible by a challenging climb from Cascade Pass, this camp is designated for those willing to earn their overnight stay via hard work.

Ross Lake Resort Cabins

Best For: Those wanting comfort and backcountry access.

Reservations: Required; book well in advance.

Amenities: kitchenettes, bedrooms, and canoe rentals

Floating on the crystal-clear waters of Ross Lake, these cabins on the water provide a unique way to experience the North Cascades. Guests can paddle out into hidden coves, fish for trout, or simply soak in the tranquility of the backcountry—without having to stay in a tent.

Wild Camping Rules and Tips

For those seeking the deepest level of solitude, wild camping (also known as dispersed camping) provides the opportunity to sleep under the stars in utter isolation.

Where Can You Wildcamp?

Outside of designated wilderness areas, scattered camping is permitted in national forests around the park.

To minimize the effect, camp at least 200 feet away from lakes, rivers, and footpaths.

Follow all fire restrictions, as much of the North Cascades is prone to wildfires.

How to Select a Safe and Responsible Site

Choose durable surfaces like rock or dry grass over soft, fragile meadows.

Camp away from animal trails and avoid places with high wildlife activity.

Always keep food in bear-proof containers or use correct hanging techniques to avoid unexpected encounters.

Wild Camping Experience

Wild camping in the North Cascades is not for beginners. There are no defined paths, amenities, or rescue services nearby. Hikers should be ready for rapid weather changes, river crossings, and unexpected wildlife encounters.

However, for those who desire pure wilderness, wild camping is one of the most gratifying ways to experience the North Cascades. Sleeping under a clear night sky, far from the sounds of civilization is an experience that makes a lasting impression on those who seek it.

Whether you want to camp alongside a glacial lake, stay in a historic fire lookout, or embark on a multi-day wild camping adventure, overnight stays in the North Cascades provide an experience unlike any other. The silence of the backcountry, the crisp mountain air, and the sheer remoteness of the wilderness all contribute to lifelong memories.

For those who prepare correctly, appreciate nature, and enjoy the adventure, a night in the North Cascades is nothing short of magical.

A Hiker's Essential Guide to Safety and Navigation in The North Cascades

The North Cascades include some of the most remote and awe-inspiring wilderness in North America. While gorgeous, this mountainous region poses serious dangers to anyone who enters it unprepared. Unlike widely visited national parks with well-marked pathways and ranger stations at every turn, the North Cascades demand self-reliance, careful planning, and a good awareness of navigation and safety measures. From reading trail signs and dealing with fast-changing weather to encountering animals and handling emergencies, knowing what to expect and how to react might be the difference between an unforgettable adventure and a dangerous misstep.

Understanding Trail Markers and Signage

Unlike some national parks, where trails are beautifully designated and easy to follow, the North Cascades necessitate a keen eye for subtle markings and a thorough understanding of navigation. Many pathways are unmaintained, washed out by seasonal floods, or partially buried by snow even in the summer months.

Trail Markers: What to Look For

Wooden Signs: At significant trail intersections, the park service has built simple wooden markers displaying the trail name and miles to the next key point. These are useful, but they should not be the main tool used for navigating.

Rock Cairns: In locations above the treeline where typical signage is impractical, hikers may find stacked rocks (cairns) indicating the proper path. While handy, cairns are not always official and might lead to confusion if moved by other hikers.

Blazes on Trees: Some pathways, especially in dense forests, use small blazes (painted or carved marks on trees) to identify the course. These are frequently faded and difficult to detect if you aren't paying carefully.

Flagging Tape: Occasionally, sections of a trail will have bright-colored tape tied to branches, especially on poorly maintained trails. These should be followed with caution, as other hikers may mark unofficial trails.

What to Do If You Lost the Trail

Even experienced hikers can lose a trail in the North Cascades. If this occurs:

Stop and analyze your surroundings. If you're not sure which way to go, don't move any farther.

Retrace your steps. Return to the last known marker or cleared portion of the trail.

Check your map and compass. Use topographic landmarks to reorient.

Look for minor clues. Worn-down bits of dirt, footsteps, or cut logs may show where the trail continues.

Never proceed blindly. If the terrain becomes hazardous, stay put and wait for better visibility or assistance.

Managing Unpredictable Weather Conditions

The weather in the North Cascades is notoriously unpredictable, ranging from clear skies to cold storms in hours. Hikers who are unprepared may find themselves in hazardous situations without warning.

Common Weather Challenges

Sudden Storms: Even in the height of summer, cold fronts can bring heavy rain, hail, and even snow at high elevations.

Dense Fog: Some of the park's ridgelines and summits are frequently engulfed in fog, making routes difficult to follow.

Lightning Strikes: Open ridges and exposed summits make hikers vulnerable to lightning strikes, particularly in late summer when thunderstorms are common.

Strong Winds: High-altitude locations frequently encounter strong gusts, making ridgeline walks hazardous.

Cold Nights: Even during peak summer, temperatures can drop below freezing at night in mountain zones.

Prepare for Sudden Weather Changes

Layering is essential. Bring a waterproof and wind-resistant shell, thermal layers, gloves, and a hat, even if the weather prediction appears good.

Always check predictions before heading out. The North Cascades feature microclimates, so the forecast for one valley may not apply just a few miles away.

Avoid exposed places during storms. If you get caught on a ridgeline, descend immediately to lower terrain to lessen the risk of lightning strikes.

Know when to turn back. Pushing on in risky conditions can result in hypothermia, falls, or being stranded.

Wildlife Safety for Bears, Cougars, and Other Animals

The North Cascades have a thriving ecosystem of wildlife, which includes black bears, cougars, mountain goats, and small mammals. While interactions are uncommon, understanding how to behave around these creatures is crucial to remaining safe.

Black Bear Encounters

Though not as hostile as their grizzly cousins, black bears are nevertheless formidable natural animals that must be approached with caution.

How to Lower the Risk of a Bear Encounter:

Make noise while hiking by talking, clapping, or using trekking poles to alert bears that you are coming.

Store food properly. Use bear-proof containers, and never store food inside your tent.

Maintain a safe distance. If you observe a bear, stay calm and steadily back away—never run.

Carry bear spray. In rare circumstances of aggressive behavior, bear spray is your best defense.

Cougar Awareness

Cougars (mountain lions) are rarely sighted; however, they do live in the North Cascades.

If you encounter a cougar:

Do not run. Running may cause a predator response.

Make yourself appear large by raising your arms and speaking firmly.

Slowly back away. Avoid turning your back on the animal.

If assaulted, fight back aggressively. Defend yourself with rocks, sticks, or trekking poles.

Mountain Goat Behavior

Though they appear innocent, mountain goats can be territorial and aggressive, especially near salt sources.

Do not feed or approach a goat.

Allow them plenty of space, especially if they have children.

If a goat chases you, go carefully away and avoid becoming trapped near cliffs.

Emergency Procedures and Rescue Service

Even with proper planning, anything can go wrong. Knowing how to respond to an emergency may save your life.

If You Become Lost

Stop and be calm. Panic causes poor decisions.

Check your supplies. Take inventory of food, water, and clothing.

Try retracing your steps to the last recognized landmark.

If you are truly lost, stay put. Rescuers have a better chance of discovering a stationary person.

If Anyone Is Injured

Assess severity. If the damage is minimal, stabilize and proceed with caution.

If the victim has major injuries (broken bones, unconsciousness), do not move them unless essential.

Use an emergency signal: blow a whistle three times, use a mirror to reflect sunlight, or wave brightly colored garments.

If possible, call for assistance. A satellite phone or personal locator beacon (PLB) can save lives in no-service areas.

who to contact in an emergency?

North Cascades National Park Dispatch Number: 360-854-7249

Call 911 for life-threatening emergencies

Local ranger stations provide backcountry assistance

The wild and inaccessible landscape of the North Cascades provides some of the most rewarding hiking experiences, but only for those who come prepared. Understanding trail markers, changing weather, wildlife encounters, and emergency protocols might mean the distinction between a safe, successful adventure and a dangerous situation.

For those willing to respect the landscape, pack smartly, and stay vigilant, the North Cascades provide an extraordinary wilderness experience—one that rewards preparedness, awareness, and respect for nature's unpredictable forces.

Responsible And Sustainable Hiking in The Northern Cascades

The North Cascades are among the few wild regions in the United States, with untamed peaks, old forests, and glacier-fed rivers. But the privilege of experiencing this gorgeous landscape comes with a responsibility: leave it as immaculate as we found it. As outdoor recreation expands, the impact of human activity becomes increasingly obvious. From trampled meadows and littered campsites to wildlife disturbances and erosion, irresponsible behavior endangers the very beauty that draws people here in the first place. Responsible hiking is more than just appreciating nature; it's also about protecting it for future generations.

Hikers may help to keep the North Cascades wild, unspoiled, and thriving for years to come by following Leave No Trace principles, respecting Indigenous lands, adopting eco-friendly hiking behaviors, and supporting conservation efforts.

Leave No Trace Principles

The Leave No Trace (LNT) framework is considered the gold standard for good outdoor ethics. It outlines specific, actionable ways to reduce human impact while conserving the wilderness experience for all.

Plan and prepare.

Before setting out, check trail conditions, rules, and weather forecasts.

Stay on approved trails to protect endangered habitats.

Bring maps, food, and suitable gear to avoid the need for emergency rescues, which put a load on park resources.

Travel and camp on durable surfaces.

Stay on established routes, rock, or gravel rather than meandering through alpine meadows or marshy areas, which might take decades to recover from erosion.

To protect water quality, camp at designated sites or, if scattered, at least 200 feet away from lakes and streams.

Dispose of waste properly

Pack out anything you bring in, including food scraps and toilet paper; even biodegradable products can take years to disintegrate in alpine regions.

For human waste, utilize a portable toilet system or dig a 6-inch kitty hole at least 200 feet away from water sources. In certain regions, garbage disposal bags are mandatory.

Leave What You Find.

Resist the impulse to pick wildflowers, collect rocks, or carve initials onto trees.

Artifacts, such as antique mining tools or Indigenous petroglyphs, should be preserved because they have historical relevance.

Reduce Campfire Impact

Because of the risk of flames and a paucity of firewood, campfires are prohibited in much of the North Cascades' high alpine zones.

Use a lightweight backpacking stove instead. If fires are permitted, use the existing fire rings and only burn little, dead wood.

Respect wildlife.

Never approach, feed, or try to touch wild animals.

Store food in bear-proof containers or use suitable hanging techniques to keep bears from connecting humans with food.

Observe wildlife from a safe distance—binoculars are an excellent tool for watching animals without upsetting them.

Be considerate of other visitors

Keep noise levels low and let nature supply the soundtrack.

Allow uphill hikers to pass and make way for faster-moving groups.

If camping, set up away from trails and other campers to maintain the woods' solitude.

Respect for Local Communities and Indigenous Lands

Indigenous people lived, traveled, and stewarded this region for thousands of years before it was designated as North Cascades National Park. Today, the Upper Skagit, Nooksack, Swinomish, Sauk-Suiattle, and other tribal nations have strong cultural ties to the mountains, rivers, and valleys.

Hikers play an important part in honoring and respecting Indigenous lands by remembering the history, customs, and rights of the original occupants.

Recognize Indigenous Presence

Learn about the tribal history of the area you're trekking in. Many paths retrace traditional Indigenous pathways used for hunting, fishing, and seasonal migration.

Encourage indigenous-led conservation activities that prioritize the protection of holy sites and natural resources.

Respect for Cultural Sites

Avoid damaging petroglyphs, ancient campsites, or burial grounds—these regions are very spiritual and historically significant.

When visiting reserve lands or tribal-owned enterprises, follow established guidelines and request permission as needed.

Supporting Local Community

Many small villages in the North Cascades rely on ecotourism. Buying from local outfitters, staying in family-owned lodges, and dining at small restaurants all contribute to the sustainability of these communities.

Be careful of how your visit affects local resources, such as garbage management and transportation, particularly in smaller communities.

Environmentally Friendly Hiking Practices

Hikers have the chance to reduce their environmental impact by making conscious decisions before, during, and after their excursion.

Reduce waste

Avoid single-use plastics and carry reusable containers, water bottles, and cutlery.

Choose minimal-packaging food to reduce unnecessary waste.

If you use energy bars or snack wrappers, keep them in a designated waste bag until they can be properly disposed of.

Use Sustainable Gear.

Invest in robust, high-quality equipment that will survive for years rather than add to rapid consumer waste.

Encourage brands to prioritize eco-friendly materials, ethical sourcing, and sustainable manufacturing practices.

Respect the land's carrying capacity

Consider hiking during the off-season to reduce traffic on popular trails.

Take lesser-known routes rather than popular ones to reduce the danger of erosion and ecosystem harm.

Carpool or take public transportation

Lower your carbon footprint by sharing rides to trailheads or taking public transportation when available.

Some localities have shuttle services, which assist reduce emissions and congestion.

Conservation Efforts in the North Cascades

Climate change, wildfires, habitat loss, and increased human activity all pose continual threats to the North Cascades. Several organizations labor intensively to protect and repair the park's endangered ecosystems.

Safeguarding Glaciers and Water Sources

The North Cascades include more than 300 glaciers, but climate change has resulted in fast ice loss, harming rivers, drinking water, and wildlife habitats.

Hikers may lower their carbon footprint by choosing low-emission transportation and supporting policies that protect public lands.

Habitat Restoration and Rewilding

The National Park Service and conservation organizations have been trying to restore damaged habitats, reintroduce native plant species, and safeguard endangered wildlife.

Visitors can help these efforts by sticking to approved trails and volunteering for trail repair programs.

Wildlife Protection

The North Cascades provide vital habitat for grizzly bears, wolves, wolverines, and other species.

Supporting organizations such as the North Cascades Institute and Conservation Northwest help to finance study and advocacy for these species.

How Hikers Can Help

Consider donating to conservation groups dedicated to preserving the North Cascades.

Participate in trail clean-up days or backcountry restoration projects.

Contact Park rangers if you witness any illegal activity, such as poaching or habitat degradation.

Responsible hiking in the North Cascades isn't simply about following rules—it's about instilling a profound appreciation for the land. By minimizing our effect, preserving Indigenous history, and embracing sustainable practices, we can ensure that these mountains, valleys, and rivers remain untouched for future generations.

For those who truly love the wilderness, the greatest way to demonstrate it is to tread softly, leave no trace, and give back to the land that has given us so much in return.

Seasonal Hiking in The North Cascades: A Guide to The Best Trails All Year Long

The North Cascades change considerably with each season, providing hikers with a unique experience based on the time of year. This region has something special to offer year-round, from lush, wildflower-filled meadows in summer to golden larches in fall, deep snowfields in winter, and thundering waterfalls in spring. However, hiking conditions vary greatly depending on the season. Weather, trail accessibility, wildlife activity, and safety concerns change throughout the year, so hikers must plan and arrive prepared.

For those who want to explore the North Cascades in all seasons, this guide breaks down the ideal times to visit, highlighting what to anticipate, where to go, and how to stay safe.

Summer Hiking (June to September): Peak Season for Adventure*

Summer is when the North Cascades come alive. As the snow melts at higher elevations, routes become fully accessible, rivers flow strongly with glacial melt, and alpine meadows explode into color with wildflowers.

What to Expect this Summer

Long daylight hours allow for great full-day hikes and multi-day hiking expeditions.

Trail accessibility has reached its peak, with even the most isolated sections becoming passable by July.

Wildflowers peak from mid-July to early August, covering the meadows in purple, yellow, and crimson.

Glacial lakes are at their most brilliant, with turquoise waters mirroring the surrounding peaks.

Best Summer Hikes

Maple Pass Loop- One of the most magnificent high-alpine walks, with wide-open mountain views and vibrant meadows.

Sahale Arm - A difficult but rewarding hike with awe-inspiring views and opportunities to observe mountain goats.

Cascade Pass: A historic trail leading into the heart of the park that provides panoramic views and access to Sahale Glacier Camp.

Hidden Lake Lookout - For those willing to brave the difficult terrain, this climb leads to a fire lookout with some of the greatest views in the Cascades.

Safety Tips for Summer

Bring lots of water—many streams dry up later in the season.

Be prepared for unpredictable weather—while summer is often mild, sudden storms can blow in swiftly at high elevations.

Begin early to avoid the heat—afternoon temperatures can be high, particularly in exposed regions.

Fall Foliage and Autumn Hiking (September to November): A Season of Color

As summer ends, the North Cascades transform into a breathtaking display of fall color, making autumn one of the greatest times to walk. With fewer tourists and cool mountain air, September and October provide some of the best hiking conditions of the year.

What To Expect in the Fall?

Larch trees turn a dazzling gold between late September and early October, making high-alpine treks exceptionally beautiful.

Cooler temperatures result in more comfortable trekking conditions, but days become shorter.

Less crowded trails, especially after mid-September, when summer tourists disperse.

Early snowfall can occur at higher elevations, as early as October.

Best Fall Hikes

Blue Lake Trails - A moderately easy hike with a breathtaking display of golden larches against a mountain backdrop.

The Rainy Pass to Heather-Maple Pass Loop is one of the best fall hikes in the North Cascades, with high ridgelines clothed in autumn colors.

Cutthroat Pass - A moderate hike that leads to incredible vistas of craggy peaks surrounded by golden larches.

Thornton Lakes and Trapper Peak - A less-traveled route with **beautiful fall colors and opportunities for solitude.

Safety Tips for Fall

Check the weather frequently; early snowfall can make routes slick and perilous.

Pack additional layers—temperatures can drop quickly, particularly in the evenings.

Begin hikes earlier—the daylight hours diminish dramatically in late September.

Winter Hiking and Snowshoeing (December to March): A Frozen Wonderland

Winter turns the North Cascades into a panorama of heavy snow, frozen waterfalls, and sparkling peaks. While typical hiking becomes challenging, snowshoeing and winter trekking provides an opportunity to explore the environment in a completely new way.

What to expect in winter?

Most trails are only accessible with snowshoes or skis due to heavy snowfall.

Low-elevation hikes remain open, allowing visitors to explore the woodlands and river basins.

Avalanche risk is substantial in alpine areas, necessitating adequate training and equipment.

Silence and solitude: winter is the least populated season in the North Cascades.

The Best Winter Snowshoe Trails

Artist Point - One of the most picturesque winter destinations, with incredible views of Mount Baker and Mount Shuksan.

Thunder Creek Trail- An excellent lower-elevation option for those who want to explore the winter woods.

Diablo Lake Overlook Although the walk itself is snow-covered, this drive-up viewpoint provides a bizarre frozen landscape.

Hannegan Pass - For experienced winter travelers, this path passes through a snowy wonderland with breathtaking mountain views.

Winter Safety Tips

Check avalanche conditions before entering the backcountry; many areas are prone to slides.

Dress in moisture-wicking and insulating layers; hypothermia is a significant risk in cold weather.

Pack the Ten Essentials, which include additional food, emergency shelter, and a headlamp.

Spring Hiking and Wildflower Trails (March-May): The Rebirth of the Wilderness

As the snow melts, the North Cascades awaken from winter's grip, and lower-elevation routes become Lush and vibrant, with new foliage and gushing waterfalls.

What To Expect in Spring?

Lowland trails open first, with higher routes remaining snow-covered long into June.

Waterfalls are at their most powerful, fuelled by melting snow on the peaks.

Mosquitoes start to appear later in the season, especially around lakes and marshlands.

Some paths remain snowbound, necessitating the use of microspikes or gaiters to ensure safe passage.

Best Spring Hikes

Thunder Knob Trail - An excellent early-season choice with views of Diablo Lake's deep blue waters.

Skagit River Loop Trail - A gentle, forested hike that provides a chance to witness wildlife emerging from winter.

Cascade Pass (early season section) - While the entire path may still be covered in snow, the lower switchbacks are frequently open in May.

Ladder Creek Falls - An easy walk with powerful cascades at peak flow.

Spring Safety Tips

Be prepared for muddy and damp conditions; trails are frequently soaked with meltwater.

Look for leftover snow at higher elevations, even in late May.

Check for road and trail closures**; certain areas are inaccessible until early summer.

The North Cascades provide a fresh adventure with each season, making it one of the most exciting and rewarding hiking destinations in the country. Whether you're looking for wildflowers in the spring, climbing high-alpine climbs in the summer, admiring golden larches in the fall, or snowshoeing through a winter wonderland, there is always something amazing waiting to be discovered.

Hiking in the North Cascades becomes a lifelong experience for those ready to accept the unique challenges and benefits of each season.

Family And Group Hiking in The North Cascades: A Guide to Safe and Memorable Experiences

Hiking in the North Cascades is a transformative experience, and sharing the trails with family or friends makes it even more enjoyable. Whether you're introducing children to the marvels of nature, bringing a four-legged companion, or organizing a group hike, planning and knowing the dynamics of hiking together can make for a smooth and pleasurable journey.

Unlike solo hikes, family and group adventures necessitate a different degree of planning and awareness—selecting the appropriate paths, ensuring everyone's comfort, adhering to trail etiquette, and emphasizing safety. This guide includes family-friendly routes, pet-friendly hiking ideas, and best practices for group hikes to ensure that everyone, from babies to seasoned adventurers, has a wonderful time in the North Cascades.

Top Family-Friendly Trails: Easy and Engaging Hikes for All Ages

Hiking with children or less experienced hikers necessitates gentle trails with rewarding views, where the excursion is exciting without being unduly strenuous. These paths have short distances, scenic stops, and interactive components such as lakes, waterfalls, or wildlife sightings.

Rainy Lake Trail

Distance: 2 kilometers round way.

Elevation Gain: Minimal.

Why it's fantastic: A paved and stroller-friendly path leads to a stunning alpine lake surrounded by high peaks. Ideal for small children or families seeking a gentle, peaceful walk.

Blue Lake Trail

Distance: 4.4-mile round trip.

Elevation Gain: 1,050 ft.

Why it's great: A modest trail leads to a magnificent turquoise lake, with wildflowers in summer and golden larches in autumn. The reasonable distance and rewarding landscape make it ideal for families with older children.

Thunder Knob Trail

Distance: 3.6-mile round trip.

Elevation Gain: 635 ft.

Why it's great: The peak offers panoramic views of Diablo Lake, and the trail's gentle incline makes it accessible to a diverse range of hikers.

Ladder Creek Falls

Distance: 0.5-mile round trip.

Elevation Gain: Minimal.

Why it's great: This short but magical trail leads through a forested canyon to a cascading waterfall, with colorful nightly illumination displays adding to the ambiance.

Washington Pass Overlook

Distance: 0.3-mile round trip.

Elevation Gain: Negative.

Why it's great: Although more of a scenic promenade than a trek, this quick walk to an elevated platform provides breathtaking views of Liberty Bell Mountain and the surrounding peaks, making it an easy yet rewarding visit for families.

Tips for Hiking with Children

Let them pick the pace. Rushing might irritate; instead, let younger walkers explore at their leisure.

Include games. To keep youngsters interested, look for animal footprints, odd rocks, or distinctive bird calls.

Bring plenty of snacks. Energy levels decrease quickly, and tiny treats can help keep the enthusiasm going.

Pack extra layers. The weather in the mountains can change fast, so even on a beautiful day, carry jackets and gloves.

Hiking with Pets: Rules and Tips for Exploring with Your Dog

Bringing a dog on the trail is a fantastic way to bond while enjoying the outdoors, but you must understand the rules and best practices to protect the safety of both your pet and the surrounding environment.

Dog-Friendly Trails in North Cascades

Many trails in the National Park are dog-free, however, the surrounding national forests and recreation areas include some pet-friendly paths.

Some recommended dog-friendly trails are:

Thunder Knob Trail (dogs are allowed on leashes)

Ross Dam Trail (a picturesque, moderately easy hike with excellent lake views)

Cutthroat Pass (for more adventurous dogs and owners).

Rules of Hiking with Dogs

Always keep your dog on a leash—this protects local wildlife, avoids conflicts with other hikers, and keeps your dog safe from cliffs or rushing water.

Pick up after your pet. Bring trash bags and put everything away, as dog waste can affect the environment.

Ensure your dog is trail-ready. Some routes include steep rock scrambles, fast-moving rivers, or spiky volcanic rock; examine trail conditions to ensure your dog can manage the terrain.

Pack extra water. Even in milder weather, dogs can quickly dehydrate. Many North Cascades streams contain glacial silt or bacteria, so pack a portable filter or additional bottled water for your dog.

Respect other hikers. Not everyone is comfortable with dogs, so step aside and give others space, especially on narrow routes.

Group Hiking Etiquette and Safety: Making the Experience Fun and Organized

Hiking in a group enhances camaraderie and shared memories, but it also entails added obligations. Larger groups have a different influence on trails than solitary hikers, therefore following proper etiquette and safety precautions ensures that everyone enjoys the trip without upsetting others or the environment.

Best Practices for Group Hikes

Stick Together, but Allow Personal Space

Instead of rushing forward, maintain a pace that is appropriate for the slowest hiker.

If the group disperses, designate checkpoints where everyone can gather.

Be mindful of noise levels

Conversations and laughter are enjoyable, but loud screaming, music, or excessive noise can disturb wildlife and other hikers.

If you use a speaker for music, leave it at home; nature offers its soundtrack.

Give preference to smaller groups and solo hikers

Large groups should move aside to allow smaller parties to pass, especially on narrow trails or steep sections.

Designate a Trail Leader and Sweep

The leader sets the pace and looks for trail markers, while the sweep stays in the back to ensure no one falls behind.

Communicate clearly

If traversing rivers, rough portions, or exposed ridges, discuss the problems ahead to keep the group informed.

Use hand signals in situations where wind or distance makes it difficult to hear.

Safety Tips for Group Hiking

Make a plan before leaving. Determine the route, turnaround time, and emergency procedures.

Carry additional supplies. A larger group equals more responsibility, so bring extra food, drink, and a first aid kit large enough to handle numerous injuries.

Decide on a "buddy system." Pair hikers up, especially on longer excursions, to prevent separation.

Be considerate of shared spaces. When camping, do not monopolize shelters, fire pits, or beautiful viewpoints—allow others to enjoy the space as well. Hiking in the North Cascades with family, pets, or a group elevates an already unforgettable experience to a shared adventure filled with connection, discovery, and teamwork. Whether going for an easy lake stroll with kids, hitting the trails with a four-legged buddy, or guiding a large group through alpine ridges, being mindful of the needs of others, respecting nature, and following best practices assures a safe and pleasant adventure.

The mountains welcome everyone, but the way we travel through them determines the state of future generations. By planning, observing etiquette, and prioritizing safety, hikers may share the beauty of the North Cascades while preserving its wildness for those who follow in their footsteps.

Multi-Day and Advanced Hiking Adventures in The North Cascades

For those looking for more than just a day trip, the North Cascades provide some of the most challenging and rewarding multi-day and advanced trekking experiences in North America. Whether traversing rocky ridgelines, fastpacking across remote valleys, climbing tough alpine routes, or crossing foreign boundaries, these excursions require talent, planning, and endurance. Unlike novice trails, these courses test both physical aptitude and mental resilience.

They lead to isolated backcountry environments where self-sufficiency is essential, necessitating good navigation skills, appropriate equipment, and familiarity with extreme circumstances.

For seasoned hikers ready to take on glacier-fed terrain, demanding elevation climbs, and multi-day backcountry exploration, these routes showcase the North Cascades' wildest, most untamed areas.

Hut-to-Hut Trekking in the North Cascades

Unlike the Alps, where hut-to-hut trekking is well-established, the North Cascades provide a tougher and more self-sufficient experience, with a few shelters and backcountry cabins functioning as distant outposts for multi-day treks.

What to Expect on Hut-to-Hut Trekking?

Rustic shelters rather than fully equipped huts - Unlike European trekking routes, North Cascades huts are frequently primitive, requiring hikers to bring their own food, sleeping bags, and cooking equipment.

A combination of backcountry camping and hut stays - Some trips include nights spent in historic fire lookouts, secluded ranger cottages, or alpine shelters.

Unrivaled solitude - With fewer people on these routes, the experience is distant.

Notable Hut-to-Hut Routes

The Cascade Pass-Stehekin Route

One of the most beautiful multi-day hikes in the range, this route takes hikers from Cascade Pass into the secluded Stehekin Valley, where they can stay in wilderness lodges or remote cabins before hiking or boating out.

Highlights: Stunning views of Johannesburg Mountain, glacier-fed waterfalls, and the transition from high-alpine terrain to dense forest.

Hidden Lake Lookout Overnight

While not a conventional hut-to-hut trek, this path takes you to a historic fire lookout positioned high above Hidden Lake, which provides one of the most magnificent overnight stays in the Cascades.

Ross Lake Resort to Desolation Peak

Begin at the floating cabins of Ross Lake Resort and trek up to Desolation Peak, where the famed fire lookout that Jack Kerouac manned for a summer still exists.

These trips necessitate logistical planning since many include boat access, backcountry permits, and self-sufficiency, yet they provide unrivaled access to the mountains.

Trail Running and Fastpacking: Covering Large Distances in the Backcountry

For athletes who want to push their endurance in the wild, the North Cascades offer some of the most technical and rewarding terrain for trail running and fastpacking.

The Benefits of Fastpacking

Combines lightweight backpacking with running or rapid hiking, enabling adventurers to go large distances with minimum equipment.

Increases access to isolated areas—by traveling faster, runners can explore landscapes that typical backpackers would take days to reach.

Requires exceptional fitness and intelligent packing, as carrying less weight implies foregoing some conveniences.

The Best Trail Running and Fastpacking Routes

Cascade Pass to the Sahale Arm

Distance: 12+ miles round way.

Why it's great: It's the ideal combination of runnable terrain and high-alpine exposure, with breathtaking ridgeline vistas.

Copper Ridge Loop

Distance: 34 miles.

Why it's great: This classic multi-day route is ideal for fastpackers, with steep mountains, glacier valleys, and river crossings.

Hannagan Pass to Whatcom Pass

Distance: 40+ miles.

Why it's great: This route puts endurance to the test, with steep climbs and breathtaking, lonely portions of the park.

Trail runners and fastpackers must be prepared for harsh weather changes, difficult terrain, and complete self-sufficiency, as assistance is often days away.

Alpine Hiking and Climbing Routes: Conquering Peaks

The North Cascades are often dubbed the "American Alps" for good reason: the landscape is steep, glaciated, and rugged, attracting climbers and advanced hikers from all over the world.

What Makes Alpine Hiking Here Special?

Many routes necessitate glacier travel, ice axes, and mountaineering skills—this is not just hiking; it's a high-elevation adventure.

Summits provide distant, rarely-seen views; many summits necessitate route-finding, scrambling, and technical climbing.

Weather conditions change quickly, making preparation and adequate gear necessary.

The Best Alpine Hiking and Climbing Routes

Eldorado Peak ("The Queen of the Cascades")

Distance: 7 miles roundtrip.

Elevation Gain: 6,500+ feet.

Why it's great: A traditional glacier climb that leads to a stunning knife-edge summit ridge.

Mt. Shuksan via Fisher Chimneys

Distance: 10 kilometers round trip.

Elevation Gain: 7,200 ft.

Why it's great: A combination of hiking, rock scrambling, and glacier travel, with a dramatic summit.

Forbidden Peak (West Ridge Route)

Distance: 10 kilometers round trip.

Elevation Gain: 5,400 ft.

Why it's great: This is one of North America's best alpine climbs, with exposed ridgeline climbing and breathtaking vistas.

These climbs require substantial planning, technical skills, and excellent conditions; therefore, they are best suited to experienced mountaineers or those with competent guided instruction.

Crossing into Canada: International Hiking Trails

The North Cascades border some of Canada's most stunning wilderness areas, allowing for cross-border hiking trips.

Key Considerations for International Hiking

Passports Required: The US-Canada border is strictly controlled, so hikers must have valid documentation and use official border crossings.

Permits May Be Required: Certain cross-border routes require special backcountry permits from both US and Canadian park officials.

Wildlife Regulations Differ: Canada has harsher laws regarding bear canisters and food storage; check requirements before crossing.

The Best Cross-Border Hiking Routes

Pacific Crest Trail (PCT) to Manning Park, British Columbia

Distance: 2,650+ miles (total trail) / 8+ miles (boundary segment)

Why it's great: The last stretch of the famed PCT enters Canada, going to Manning Park, a popular wilderness region.

Chilliwack Valley Loop (US-Canada Border Route)

Distance: 45 miles.

Why it's great: This remote loop traverses international borders and leads hikers through high-alpine meadows, rugged ridgelines, and glacier-fed rivers.

Ross Lake - Hozomeen Lake (Canada Border Segment)

Distance: 10 miles.

Why it's great: A breathtaking backcountry hike that follows Ross Lake northward into British Columbia and provides an off-the-grid, international hiking experience.

For those looking for a genuinely unique adventure, crossing into Canada provides an extra dimension of exploration, culture, and backcountry immersion.

The North Cascades are a playground for advanced hikers and multi-day adventurers, providing some of the most intense, breathtaking, and rewarding challenges in the Pacific Northwest. Whether taking on high-altitude climbs, long-distance fastpacking routes, or cross-border expeditions, these adventures push hikers beyond their limits and into some of the wildest, most untamed landscapes left on Earth.

The North Cascades await those who want to put their endurance, abilities, and spirit of adventure to the test.

Practical Travel Tips for Exploring the North Cascades

The North Cascades provide some of the most stunning wilderness in the Pacific Northwest, yet accessing these inaccessible peaks and valleys needs careful preparation and local knowledge. Unlike some national parks with huge visitor hubs, the North Cascades are wild and untamed, thus lodging, food, and transportation options may be limited. For those looking for an unforgettable experience—whether hiking deep into the backcountry, staying in a cozy mountain lodge, or discovering lesser-known trails—this guide covers everything you need to know about getting there, where to stay, where to eat, and how to find hidden gems away from the crowds.

Transportation to the North Cascades: Airports and Transit

Unlike many national parks with enormous, bustling gates, the North Cascades are off the beaten path and need some effort to get. The additional planning is well worth it because the payoff is a panorama of towering peaks, crystal-clear lakes, and boundless wilderness.

Nearest Airports

While the North Cascades lack a large airport, there are several possibilities within a few hours' drive.

Seattle-Tacoma International Airport (SEA) is the largest and best-served airport, with the most flight options. The park is approximately 2.5 to 3.5 hours by car away from here, depending on your destination.

Bellingham International Airport (BLI) is a tiny, regional airport located around 1.5 hours from the North Cascades.

It's an excellent choice for passengers going from West Coast cities such as Portland, San Francisco, or Los Angeles.

Vancouver overseas Airport (YVR, Canada) - If you're traveling from Canada or overseas destinations, Vancouver is a good alternative. However, crossing the border into the United States increases the duration of the trip.

Drive to the North Cascades

As public transit is limited, driving is the best method to see the region. The two main access routes are:

Highway 20 (North Cascades Highway) - The most scenic drive that runs through the center of the park. This road is seasonal and usually open from April to November.

Highway 542 (Mount Baker Highway) - The primary trailhead for hikes near Mount Baker and Artist Point.

Public Transport Options

For individuals without a car, options are limited, but feasible.

Amtrak provides train service to Mount Vernon, where passengers can rent a car.

Greyhound and FlixBus travel to towns such as Bellingham and Burlington, with rental cars accessible nearby.

North Cascades National Park Shuttle (Summer Only) - A seasonal shuttle runs from Marblemount to the Stehekin Valley and provides limited access to distant locations.

Where to Stay: Hotels, Lodges, and Cabins

Accommodations in the North Cascades range from cozy cabins and backcountry lodges to low-cost motels and camping options. However, spots fill up quickly in the summer, so book early.

North Cascades Lodges and Resorts

Ross Lake Resort - One of the most unique accommodations, this resort offers floating cabins on Ross Lake that can only be reached by boat or trekking.

Sun Mountain Lodge (Winthrop) - A luxury lodge overlooking the Methow Valley that provides gourmet meals and outdoor activities.

Freestone Inn (Mazama) is a luxurious yet rustic mountain retreat ideal for people seeking comfort near the park.

Hotels and motels

If you prefer traditional lodging, the best options are in adjacent towns:

Winthrop: A historic Western-themed town with a collection of quaint inns, including Hotel Rio Vista and Chewuch Inn & Cabins.

Marblemount: One of the closest locations to the park, featuring basic yet comfortable lodgings such as Buffalo Run Inn.

Concrete and Sedro-Woolley: Small communities with a few motels, convenient for those arriving via Highway 20.

Cabins and Unique Accommodations

Cabins provide a more secluded experience by offering seclusion and proximity to nature.

North Cascades Basecamp (Mazama) - Cozy cabins with direct trail access, perfect for hikers.

Glacier Peak Resort (Rockport) - A tranquil stay along the Skagit River, ideal for **fishing and hiking nearby.

For those who want to fully immerse themselves in the wilderness, backcountry camping or staying at a fire lookout hut are unforgettable experiences.

Where to Eat and Resupply While Hiking

The North Cascades is a remote wilderness, thus dining and grocery alternatives are limited. Stocking up before entering the park is critical, particularly for multi-day hikes.

Best Restaurants Near the Park

Mondo Restaurant (Marblemount) - A popular spot for hikers looking to feed up before or after a hike, serving hearty breakfasts and burgers.

Riverside Grill (Winthrop) - A casual restaurant with fresh, local ingredients and stunning riverfront views.

Stehekin Pastry Company (Stehekin) - A fabled bakery hidden deep in the wilderness that can only be reached by boat or trek. The cinnamon rolls and apple strudel are well worth the journey.

Milepost 111 Brewing (Cashmere) - For those returning to Seattle, this brewpub serves craft beer and delicious pub fare.

Where to Purchase Hiking Supplies and Resupply

For hikers headed on multi-day excursions, knowing where to resupply or grab last-minute gear is critical:

Winthrop Mountain Sports (Winthrop) is ideal for gear rentals, maps, and last-minute hiking needs.

Skagit Valley Food Co-op (Mount Vernon) is a high-quality grocery store with organic food and bulk trail snacks.

Mazama Store (Mazama)- A popular general store that serves homemade sandwiches, espresso, and outdoor gear.

For individuals embarking on extended thru-hikes, sending a resupply package to Stehekin via the post office can provide fresh food halfway through the journey.

Hidden Gems and Off-Beaten-Path Adventures

While the North Cascades offer many famous treks and viewpoints, those who travel off the major routes can uncover hidden trails, forgotten fire lookouts, and virgin alpine lakes.

The Secret Larches of Cutthroat Valley

While Cutthroat Pass is a popular larch trek, few people visit the surrounding Cutthroat Valley, where golden larches reflect in mirror-like alpine tarns.

Horseshoe Basin, A Remote Wilderness Haven

Located far from the crowds, this high-altitude basin provides fantastic vistas of craggy peaks, floral fields, and perfect seclusion.

Desolation Peak Fire Lookout (Without Crowds)

While Jack Kerouac made Desolation Peak famous, few hikers approach from the Hozomeen side, which provides a quieter, more satisfying route to the summit.

Cascade River Road's Forgotten Trails

While most people stop at Cascade Pass, continuing further down Cascade River Road leads to lesser-known but equally magnificent hikes, such as Eldorado Basin and Magic Mountain.

Visiting the North Cascades requires planning, but the effort is rewarded with some of the most stunning scenery in the

Pacific Northwest. Whether you're flying in, locating a nice cabin, refueling with fresh-baked pastries, or discovering a secret alpine paradise, these useful recommendations will help you make the most of your adventure.

For those who plan ahead of time and embrace the region's wild nature, the North Cascades provide an experience that lasts long after the voyage is completed.

Conclusion: The End of The Trail, But Not the Adventure

The North Cascades aren't just a location to visit—they're a scenery that makes an impression on every traveler who ventures into their harsh terrain. Whether you've stood on the brink of a glacier lake, climbed a fire lookout at daybreak, or found solitude deep in an alpine valley, this wild region of the Pacific Northwest has a way of sticking with you long after you've left. The North Cascades provide something for everyone, with soaring peaks, immense wilderness, and paths ranging from easy lakeside strolls to arduous multi-day climbs. However, despite the breathtaking panoramas, these mountains require respect, planning, and a dedication to responsible exploration.

This book includes the greatest trails, seasonal hiking tips, responsible travel practices, safety considerations, lodging, cuisine, and hidden gems. However, no written words can properly capture the emotion of being atop a ridge at sunrise, hearing the distant crack of a glacier shifting, or seeing a mountain goat perched impossibly high above a valley. The

North Cascades are better experienced rather than read about.

Final thoughts and recommendations

Whether you're a seasoned mountaineer or a first-time visitor, a well-planned journey to the North Cascades may change the way you perceive the world. Before you embark on your adventure, consider these final thoughts to guarantee it is safe, pleasurable, and unforgettable.

Select the appropriate adventure for your skill level

The North Cascades have everything from accessible, family-friendly trails to strenuous alpine routes that demand strong mountaineering skills. The key to a fun experience is to match your adventure to your experience level.

Beginners & Families: Stick to well-marked paths like Rainy Lake, Blue Lake, or Thunder Knob, where you may enjoy beautiful scenery without exerting too much effort.

Intermediate Hikers: Move on to more moderate trails such as Maple Pass Loop, Cascade Pass, or Hidden Lake Lookout, where elevation gains rewards hikers with panoramic vistas.

Advanced Explorers: Test your limits with Sahale Arm, Desolation Peak, or multi-day treks like the Copper Ridge Loop, where the genuine wilderness experience awaits.

Alpine Climbers & Fastpackers: Test your limitations on Eldorado Peak, Forbidden Peak, or the Ptarmigan Traverse, which require endurance, navigation skills, and technical competence.

If you're unsure about a trail, start with a shorter hike and work your way up—the mountains will always be there, ready for your next adventure.

Travel with awareness and respect for the land.

The North Cascades National Park is one of the least developed and wildest in the United States, which is a rare privilege. Keeping it that way means traveling responsibly, according to Leave No Trace principles, and respecting both the environment and Indigenous lands.

Pack out everything you bring in—even biodegradable food waste might harm local ecosystems.

Stay on approved trails to protect delicate alpine meadows and prevent erosion.

Respect local wildlife—allow bears, mountain goats, and other creatures their space.

Recognize the region's Indigenous history and, if feasible, support local communities.

By hiking and camping thoughtfully and responsibly, we can ensure that future generations inherit the same unspoiled landscapes that we have the opportunity to discover today.

Be prepared for the unexpected.

The North Cascades are remote, unexpected, and frequently unforgiving, which is why they are still so wild. Whether you're going on a short day hike or a weeklong backcountry expedition, be prepared for shifting conditions, unexpected obstacles, and emergencies.

Check the weather forecast, but be prepared for it to alter without notice.

Bring a thorough map, compass, and GPS device—cell service is spotty at best.

Bring extra food, water, and emergency supplies, even on short walks.

Tell someone about your itinerary before venturing into the backcountry.

Be aware of the symptoms of altitude sickness, hypothermia, and dehydration—and respond swiftly if any arise.

A well-prepared hiker is a safe hiker, and safety ensures that every trip concludes on a positive note rather than in a rescue operation.

Discover Your Hidden Gems.

While classic treks like Cascade Pass and Maple Pass are well worth the effort, some of the most satisfying experiences come from deviating from the well-worn paths and seeking out lesser-known but equally breathtaking routes.

Explore the secluded and wild Horseshoe Basin, where jagged peaks soar above pristine valleys.

Camp at Hozomeen Lake, a remote location near the Canadian border with mirror-like reflections of the surrounding cliffs.

Discover the alpine beauties of Whatcom Pass, where glaciers and ancient woods converge.

Every hiker has a unique trip, and the North Cascades reward those who seek adventure beyond the obvious.

Plan a return visit.

No single journey can encompass everything the North Cascades have to offer. With each season bringing a different perspective and dozens of trails yet to be explored, it's easy to fall in love with these mountains and keep coming back for more.

Come in the summer for high-alpine meadows blooming with wildflowers. Come in fall for golden larches and cool mountain air.

Experience a winter experience with snowshoeing and frozen lakes

Observe the waterfalls and gushing rivers of spring, when snowmelt nourishes the landscape.

Every season rewrites the tale of the North Cascades, presenting fresh obstacles and stunning views. If this is your first visit, it will not be the last.

Stay in Touch and Share Your Experiences

One of the most enjoyable aspects of enjoying the outdoors is sharing the experience with others. Every hiker's journey, whether through photographs, trail reports, or simply storytelling over a campfire, contributes to a better understanding of the natural areas we protect and cherish.

How to Stay Connected with the Hiking Community

Join an online hiking forum, such as the Washington Trails Association or North Cascades National Park organizations.

Share your trail experiences via trip reports, social media, or a personal blog.

Support conservation efforts—consider giving to or volunteering with groups that seek to protect the park.

Encourage others to explore responsibly—whether it's taking a friend on their first walk or offering safety advice, helping others enjoy the outdoors is one of the finest ways to give back.

The North Cascades have a way of bringing people together, building ties not only with nature but also with other adventurers who share your passion.

Tell Us Your Story

Have you got a favorite recollection from the North Cascades? A trail that made you speechless? A lesson learned the hard way? Sharing your story encourages people to explore the outdoors while also providing useful information about hiking responsibly.

Each hiker's experience is unique, but one thing is consistent: the mountains have a way of drawing us back.

The North Cascades are more than just a location on a map; they are a wilderness experience that sticks with you long after you leave. Whether you come for the jagged peaks, the turquoise lakes, the calm forests, or the challenge of the trails, these mountains will etch themselves into your memory.

Every time you lace on your boots and walk down a trail, you become a part of the story of this incredible area. What's the best part? There's always more to discover.

APPENDIX

The North Cascades offer breathtaking landscapes, remote wilderness, and an unparalleled sense of adventure, but a successful trip here requires proper preparation. Whether you're a first-time visitor or a seasoned traveler returning for more, having the right resources at your fingertips can make all the difference.

This appendix covers must-have travel apps, a detailed packing checklist, emergency contacts, frequently asked questions, and sample itineraries to help you make the most of your time in this spectacular region.

Useful Apps

Technology has transformed how we explore the outdoors, and while the North Cascades remain a rugged, off-the-grid destination, having the right apps can enhance your trip while keeping you safe. Here are some of the most helpful ones to download before your adventure.

Maps and Navigation

Gaia GPS - Offers detailed topographic maps, offline access, and tracking features for backcountry navigation.

AllTrails - Great for trail reviews, elevation profiles, and GPS guidance, especially for well-traveled routes.

Avenza Maps - Allows you to download official National Park Service (NPS) maps and use them offline.

onX Backcountry - Perfect for off-trail exploration, showing land boundaries, trail conditions, and terrain details.

Weather and Safety

NOAA Weather Radar - Provides accurate, real-time weather updates, including severe weather alerts.

Mountain Forecast - Offers detailed weather predictions for specific peaks and elevations in the North Cascades.

Avalanche Forecast (NWAC) - A must-have for winter hikers and climbers, providing up-to-date avalanche warnings.

Wildlife and Conservation

iNaturalist – Helps identify plants and wildlife you encounter on the trail.

Seek by iNaturalist – A fun, interactive way to learn about the flora and fauna of the region.

Travel and Logistics

Google Maps – Essential for finding trailheads, gas stations, and accommodations before heading into the backcountry.

Washington State Ferries – If your trip involves ferry routes, this app provides schedules, wait times, and ticket booking.

Communication and Safety

Garmin Explore – Pairs with Garmin inReach devices for satellite communication in areas with no cell service.

First Aid by American Red Cross – A handy app with quick-reference emergency guides for injuries, bites, and weather-related hazards.

Essential Travel Checklist for the North Cascades

Packing the right gear can make or break your experience in the North Cascades. Whether you're planning a short-day hike or a multi-day expedition, use this checklist to ensure you have everything you need.

Hiking Essentials (For Day and Multi-Day Trips)

Backpack (20-50L capacity depending on trip length)

Topographic map and compass/GPS device

Headlamp with extra batteries

Multi-tool or knife

Trekking poles (optional but helpful on steep terrain)

Clothing

Base layers (moisture-wicking, breathable fabric)

Insulating layer (fleece or down jacket for warmth)

Waterproof jacket and pants

Hiking pants and shirts (avoid cotton).

Wool or synthetic hiking socks

Hat and gloves (even in summer, high elevations can be cold)

Footwear

Waterproof hiking boots or trail shoes

Camp sandals or lightweight shoes (for relaxing at camp)

Food and Hydration

Lightweight stove and fuel (for multi-day hikes)

Collapsible bowl, utensils, and mug

High-energy snacks (trail mix, protein bars, dried fruit)

Bear-proof food container or bear hang kit

Water bottles (at least 2L per person)

Water filter or purification tablets

Safety and First Aid

First aid kit with blister treatment, bandages, and medications

Emergency shelter (lightweight bivy sack or space blanket)

Sunscreen and sunglasses.

Bug spray or head net (especially in summer months)

Whistle and signal mirror (for emergencies)

Camping Gear (For Multi-Day Adventures)

Lightweight tent or bivy sack

Sleeping bag (appropriate for nighttime temperatures)

Sleeping pad (for insulation and comfort)

Bear spray (know how to use it before heading into bear country)

Emergency Contacts for the North Cascades

Being prepared means knowing who to contact if something goes wrong. While the North Cascades are remote, help is available if you know where to find it.

Emergency Numbers

911 – For life-threatening emergencies (request **North Cascades Search and Rescue if needed).

North Cascades National Park Dispatch – (360) 854-7249.

Washington State Patrol (Sedro-Woolley Office) - (360) 428-3200

National Park Service Information Line - (360) 854-7200

Local Hospitals

PeaceHealth United General Medical Center (Sedro-Woolley) - Closest hospital to the west side of the park.

Three Rivers Hospital (Brewster) - Closest medical facility on the eastern side.

Road and Trail Conditions

Washington State DOT Road Conditions - (800) 695-ROAD or visit wsdot.wa.gov

North Cascades Trail Conditions - Check the National Park Service website or call a ranger station.

Frequently Asked Questions

When is the best time to visit the North Cascades?

June through September offers the best conditions for hiking, with wildflower blooms, clear trails, and warm temperatures.

October brings stunning fall colors, while winter is ideal for snowshoeing and backcountry skiing.

Do I need a permit for hiking and camping?

Day hikes do not require permits but backcountry camping does. Popular areas like Sahale Glacier Camp require reservations.

Is there cell service in the park?

Cell service is limited or non-existent in most of the park. Always carry a map, GPS, or satellite communication device if heading into remote areas.

Are there bears in the North Cascades?

Yes. Black bears are common, and grizzly bears have been spotted in remote areas. Carry bear spray, store food properly, and know **how to respond to an encounter.

Can I bring my dog?

Dogs are not allowed on most trails in the national park but are permitted in the surrounding national forests. Check trail regulations before bringing a pet.

Travel Itineraries

3-Day Itinerary: Classic Highlights

Day 1: Drive North Cascades Highway, hike Thunder Knob Trail, and camp at Colonial Creek.

Day 2: Hike Cascade Pass & Sahale Arm, and enjoy the sunset at Diablo Lake Overlook.

Day 3: Explore Rainy Lake & Blue Lake, then return via Winthrop for food and lodging.

5-Day Itinerary: Deeper Exploration

Days 1-2: Copper Ridge Loop or Hidden Lake Lookout overnight.

Day 3: Rest Day in Winthrop, visit Sun Mountain Lodge.

Day 4: Hike Maple Pass Loop, return to camp or lodge.

Day 5: Explore Stehekin, ferry on Lake Chelan, or return home.

7-Day Itinerary: Ultimate Adventure

Days 1-3: Multi-day trek (Sahale Arm or Ptarmigan Traverse).

Days 4-5: Basecamp in Winthrop, explore cutthroat larch hikes.

Days 6-7: Alpine climbing in the Mount Baker area, or relax at Ross Lake Resort.

A well-planned trip to the North Cascades is the key to an unforgettable experience. Whether you're tackling a short scenic hike or venturing deep into the backcountry, being prepared ensures a safe, rewarding, and breathtaking adventure.

Made in United States
Troutdale, OR
07/08/2025